CW00924442

100 Ideas for
Secondary Teachers:

Outstanding Computing
Lessons

Other titles in the 100 Ideas for Secondary Teachers series:

100 Ideas for Secondary Teachers:

Outstanding Computing Lessons

Simon Johnson

BLOOMSBURY EDUCATION

LONDON   OXFORD   NEW YORK   NEW DELHI   SYDNEY

BLOOMSBURY EDUCATION
Bloomsbury Publishing Plc
50 Bedford Square, London, WC1B 3DP, UK
29 Earlsfort Terrace, Dublin 2, Ireland

BLOOMSBURY, BLOOMSBURY EDUCATION and the Diana logo are
trademarks of Bloomsbury Publishing Plc

First published in Great Britain 2021

Text copyright © Simon Johnson, 2021

Simon Johnson has asserted his right under the Copyright, Designs and
Patents Act, 1988, to be identified as Author of this work

Bloomsbury Publishing Plc does not have any control over, or responsibility
for, any third-party websites referred to or in this book. All internet addresses
given in this book were correct at the time of going to press. The author and
publisher regret any inconvenience caused if addresses have changed or sites
have ceased to exist, but can accept no responsibility for any such changes

All rights reserved. No part of this publication may be reproduced or
transmitted in any form or by any means, electronic or mechanical, including
photocopying, recording, or any information storage or retrieval system,
without prior permission in writing from the publishers

A catalogue record for this book is available from the British Library

ISBN: PB: 978-1-4729-8440-1; ePDF: 978-1-4729-8442-5;
ePub: 978-1-4729-8441-8

2 4 6 8 10 9 7 5 3   (paperback)

Typeset by Newgen KnowledgeWorks Pvt. Ltd., Chennai, India
Printed and bound in the UK by CPI Group Ltd, Croydon CR0 4YY

To find out more about our authors and books visit www.bloomsbury.com
and sign up for our newsletters

Contents

Acknowledgements

This book would not have been possible without the help and support of the following people:

Thank you to my editor at Bloomsbury, Hannah Marston, for believing in me and helping me to fulfil a lifelong dream of becoming a published author.

A huge thank-you must also go to all the kind and supportive members of #caschat who, every Tuesday night on Twitter, generously impart their knowledge and experience freely for the benefit of the subject. Many of the ideas in this book owe their inclusion thanks to conversations that started on Twitter.

Thank you to all the incredible people who have kindly given permission for me to share their ideas or have shared their work freely under a Creative Commons Licence:

IDEA 38. Features of a CPU (a lesson using DART) – John Bilton, @jonbilton http://johnbiltoncomputing.blogspot.com/2013/04/win-lose-or-draw.html

IDEA 44. Crazy characters – Barefoot Computing, @BarefootComp www.barefootcomputing.org/resources/crazy-character-algorithms

IDEA 52. Image compression – @csunplugged https://classic.csunplugged.org/image-representation

IDEA 55. The intelligent piece of paper (AI) – @csunplugged https://classic.csunplugged.org/artificial-intelligence

IDEA 59. How computers work – Gary Kacmarcik http://cse4k12.org/how_computers_work/index.html

IDEA 60. Memory – Philip Upstone https://community.computingatschool.org.uk/resources/938/single

IDEA 97. Turtle snowflakes – Raspberry Pi Foundation projects.raspberrypi.org/en/projects/turtle-snowflakes

And last, but not least, thank you to my wonderful wife, Helen, for her support and encouragement while I was writing this book.

Introduction

I firmly believe that computer science is for everyone. Not only does it foster problem-solving, creativity and critical thinking skills, but it also has the potential to empower young people and give them the tools to express themselves in a variety of cool ways.

As society becomes increasingly more reliant on the use of technology, the need for a formal computing education or qualification becomes ever more important. Not only are we preparing students for the digital world, but we are also preparing them for jobs that don't even exist yet. It is therefore imperative that we provide our students with the necessary tools to prepare them for every opportunity that might come their way.

Writing this book gave me the opportunity to reflect on my own teaching practice. It reminded me that, despite graduating with honours in computer science, the thought of teaching computing for the first time filled me with trepidation. However, I was also reminded of how excited I was at the prospect of being able to try out some new teaching strategies, in particular, the idea of teaching computing without computers (also known as 'teaching unplugged').

I was also able to reflect on the valuable lessons learned while teaching computing, probably the most notable being that context is key! By making computing relevant and providing a 'real-life' context, you can create meaningful learning experiences for your students. This also applies to relating computing content to other aspects of the curriculum, which is why I have dedicated a chapter in this book to STEAM (science, technology, engineering, arts and mathematics).

I also learned that you should never be afraid to let your students teach you! One of the biggest mistakes that I made early on in my teaching career was to assume that I must be the fount of all knowledge. The truth of the matter is that it's impossible to know everything, especially with a subject like computing. In fact, there will be times when your students know more than you – coming to terms with this inevitable truth is an important step in your professional development. Be open to learning alongside your students and don't be afraid to ask them for help!

Finally, despite what the title of the book may suggest, the intention of this book is not to make every lesson outstanding. While it is admirable to aspire to be outstanding all the time, to achieve this would be unsustainable and a detriment to your health and wellbeing! Instead, this book is a compilation of tried and tested practical ideas, designed to be adapted and modified, which have the potential to create outstanding learning experiences for you and your students.

I would love to hear how you use these ideas in your own classroom, so please do get in touch! Please share your reflections with me @clcsimon on Twitter using the #100ideas hashtag or via my Facebook page, www.facebook.com/teachwithict.

How to use this book

This book includes quick, easy and practical ideas for you to dip in and out of to help you deliver effective and engaging computing lessons.

Each idea includes:

- a catchy title, easy to refer to and share with your colleagues
- an interesting quote linked to the idea
- a summary of the idea in bold, making it easy to flick through the book and identify an idea you want to use at a glance
- a step-by-step guide to implementing the idea.

Each idea also includes one or more of the following:

Teaching tip

Practical tips and advice for how and how not to run the activity or put the idea into practice.

Taking it further

Ideas and advice for how to extend the idea or develop it further.

Bonus idea ★

There are 50 bonus ideas in this book that are extra-exciting, extra-original and extra-interesting.

Share how you use these ideas and find out what other practitioners have done using **#100ideas**.

Online resources accompany this book at **www.bloomsbury.com/100-ideas-secondary-computing**. Here you will find editable versions of all the code needed to run the ideas. You can copy and paste the code or tweak it to suit your requirements. There are also a variety of downloadable resources such as pre-prepared cards and worksheets to help you put the ideas into practice.

Programming strategies

Part 1

Paired programming

'Sir, is it my turn to drive yet?'

For many, the idea of students working in pairs at a computer, especially if access to a computer is limited, is fairly common. However, even if you have the luxury of students being able to work on their own at a computer, you may still wish to consider students working in pairs, particularly when learning how to code.

Teaching tip

Switch roles regularly to ensure that all the students get a fair share of being both driver and navigator. I find that setting a timer/alarm for five-minute intervals helps to manage the students' time effectively and keeps them engaged!

Paired programming, as the name suggests, sees students working in pairs, with one taking the role of the driver (inputting the code into the computer) and the other assuming the role of navigator (reading out instructions and checking each line of code as it is typed in).

Pairing students up makes sense for a number of reasons, even more so when learning how to code! Paired programming has been shown to improve overall confidence, produce fewer errors and increase engagement compared with learning to code individually. In fact, it is a practice that is widely used in industry by professional programmers.

A word of caution! While at first it may seem beneficial to pair up higher-achieving students with those of lower ability, I find that this can have negative effects, as often one student may feel that they are being held back or another may take over completely. Experience shows that pairing students of similar ability seems to produce the best outcomes.

Rubber duck debugging

'I name my duck Ducky McDuck Face!'

Have you ever started asking someone to help you to solve a problem and, halfway through, you figure it out for yourself? Well, this is pretty much how rubber duck debugging works. The majority of 'code bugs' originate from not being clear and explicit with instructions. By describing your problem to the duck, you force yourself to express your ideas in a clear and logical way!

Rubber duck debugging is a programming methodology used by software engineers to help them to find bugs and problems in their code. The term 'rubber duck' refers to an inanimate object that understands little or nothing about the given problem!

First, you'll need to acquire some rubber ducks! I find that the local pound store is usually a good place to start. Give each student a duck and ask them to name it. Once the students have named their duck and have stopped throwing them around the classroom (!), ask them to place their duck next to their computer. Tell the students to address their duck by its name and tell the duck something about themselves – while feeling strange at first, this should help the students to get over the fear of talking to the duck in front of their peers!

Share with students some broken code (I tend to start with some simple syntax errors) and a brief explanation of what the code is meant to do. Tell the students to inform their duck that they're going to go over some code with it! Instruct the students to explain to their duck what the code is supposed to do and then explain the code in detail (line by line).

Eventually, the students should spot the seemingly obvious error, at which point they can thank their duck for being such a help!

Teaching tip

Despite what the name suggests, you don't have to use a rubber duck. Any inanimate object will suffice: a can of pop, a hat, a scarf or even a favourite teddy!

Code golf

'Anyone for a game of code golf? Fore!'

One strategy that exemplifies the concept of gamification in the teaching of coding is a game called 'code golf'.

Teaching tip

To make the challenge fair and consistent, I recommend that you set some competition rules. For example:

- Blank lines do not count as lines of code.
- Comments do not count as lines of code.
- Importing libraries do not count as lines of code.
- Everything else counts.

Code golf owes its name to its resemblance to the scoring system used in conventional golf, where participants aim to achieve the lowest score possible. The idea is simple: participants are given a problem (or working solution) and are challenged to solve it using the fewest lines of code.

The aim of code golf is to encourage efficient use of code. Efficient code uses less RAM, compiles faster and uses up less storage space. Students can use a combination of features such as loops (for, while, repeat) and functions (or sub-routines) to achieve their optimised code. However, readability and usability must not be sacrificed at the expense of code optimisation. Therefore, white space and comments do not count as lines; we still want to encourage students to break up and comment their code so that it is comprehensible to others, easier to debug and easy for others to reuse.

There are two main ways to play code golf. The first way requires students to solve a given problem using the fewest lines of code. The second method, which requires a little more preparation from the teacher, requires the students to optimise a given working solution. In both methods, the challenge is for the students to create a solution using the least amount of code. To add a little extra challenge, the teacher can add a 'par' value (or target number), with the par being the optimal number of lines of code. This par value can be altered for different levels of ability (similar to the 'handicap' system in conventional golf), thus allowing the teacher to differentiate the activity.

The following is an example of a simple 'par challenge' using the turtle library in Python. In this example, students are challenged to create a square using six lines of code (par 6). Share the following example code and ask the students to identify the repeating pattern.

```
import turtle #Import the turtle library
#Create a new window
window = turtle.Screen()
#Create a new turtle called timmy
timmy = turtle.Turtle()
timmy.forward(100)
timmy.right(90)
timmy.forward(100)
timmy.right(90)
timmy.forward(100)
timmy.right(90)
timmy.forward(100)
timmy.right(90)
```

Ask students to suggest ways in which the code can be made more efficient – draw out answers such as 'use a loop' or 'use a repeat', etc. Share the optimised solution for the above example:

```
import turtle #Import the turtle library
#Create a new window
window = turtle.Screen()
#Create a new turtle called timmy
timmy = turtle.Turtle()
for loopCounter in range(4):
    timmy.forward(100)
    timmy.right(90)
```

Inform the students that, in the modified example, the code has been made more efficient by using a counted loop. Explain that efficient code uses less RAM, compiles faster and uses up less storage space.

Put students into pairs (see Idea 1: Paired programming) and challenge them to create a series of regular polygon shapes (e.g. equilateral triangle, pentagon, hexagon, etc.) using the fewest lines of code possible.

Bonus idea ★

Create a score card for students to record the number of lines used for each shape.

Game design

'Miss, can we make Flappy Bird?'

Often, the first time that you mention the word 'coding' to children, their initial reaction is 'are we going to make games?'. While coding is not about making games, game design can be used as a hook to encourage students to learn to code.

Taking it further

Many game-creation tools allow you to add your own sprites and graphics. I find that this provides a perfect opportunity to explore Creative Commons and encourage students to design their own game sprites.

Game design, as the name suggests, is the process of planning the content and rules of a game. It also includes the design of gameplay, environment, storyline and even characters. Now, thanks to a plethora of free online tools, coding games has never been easier!

Scratch (scratch.mit.edu) is perfect for creating games and, despite its simplicity and appeal to younger audiences, should be on everyone's list of 'go-to' game-creation tools.

Stencyl (www.stencyl.com) is a free game-creation platform, which, utilising a Scratch-like interface, allows students to create games for iOS, Android, Windows and Mac.

Alice (www.alice.org) is a free and open-source 3D-programming environment designed to teach students object-oriented and event-driven programming. In Alice, students drag and drop graphic tiles in order to create animations or program simple games in 3D.

App Inventor (appinventor.mit.edu) is a great tool to teach programming. Like Scratch, App Inventor uses a drag-and-drop interface that allows you to assemble code from blocks.

Microsoft MakeCode Arcade (arcade. makecode.com) is a web-based, beginner-friendly code editor that allows you to create retro arcade games. With MakeCode Arcade, students can create games using either blocks, JavaScript or a combination of both.

PRIMM

'My students seem so much more confident when learning to code using PRIMM.'

PRIMM incorporates discussion and investigation of sample code through scaffolded tasks to help students to understand code before they start writing their own code.

I was first introduced to the idea of PRIMM at a Computing at School workshop led by Dr Sue Sentence (King's College London).

PRIMM is a research-based approach to teaching programming. It is made up of five stages: Predict, Run, Investigate, Modify, Make. Each stage is used in planning lessons and activities to support the learning of programming.

The five stages of PRIMM are:

- **Predict:** Students are given a working program and challenged to predict what the code will do. At this level, the focus is on what the code actually does.
- **Run:** Students run the program so that they can test their predictions and discuss their findings with their partner or the rest of the class.
- **Investigate:** The teacher provides a range of scaffolded activities aimed to help the students to explore what each line of code does. Strategies can include tracing, commenting code, annotating, debugging, etc.
- **Modify:** Students are challenged to modify the working program in order to change its functionality in some way.
- **Make:** Students design a new program that is based on the given solution but which solves a new problem.

> **Teaching tip**
>
> It is not expected that you cover all five stages in one lesson. In fact, you may wish to focus on one stage over several lessons.

IDEA 6

Parsons problems

'Help students to learn how to code by removing some of the barriers!'

When students move from block-based languages to text-based languages, they often get frustrated with syntax errors. One method that helps to reduce this frustration is 'Parsons problems'.

Teaching tip

You don't need a computer to introduce Parsons problems. I find that eliminating computers altogether can further reduce confusion and frustration! I suggest starting by printing and laminating some code blocks or lines of code for students to sort.

Parsons problems are programming puzzles where a working solution to a problem has been broken up into blocks of code and jumbled up. Students are given the mixed-up code and challenged to reassemble the code in the correct order.

Some Parsons problems, often referred to as two-dimensional Parsons problems, also require the code blocks to be indented correctly. Parsons problems can also contain extra lines of code, called distractors, which are not needed for the code to work.

Although primarily used with text-based languages, Parsons problems can be used with block-based languages too! The idea is to allow students to focus on the core concepts, such as flow of control, conditionals and loops, without the frustration of syntax errors.

Example of a Parsons problem with distractors:

Parsons problem
```
timmy = turtle.Turtle()
window = turtle.Screen()
timmy.forward(100)
timmy.right(90)
timmy.turn(90)
For loopCounter in range(4)
for loopCounter in range(4):
import turtle
```

Solution
```
import turtle
window = turtle.Screen()
timmy = turtle.Turtle()
for loopCounter in range(4):
    timmy.forward(100)
    timmy.right(90)
```

Use-modify-create

'Reduce anxiety while supporting growth with this simple three-stage approach to learning to code!'

When we learn to read and write as children, we often tend to learn how to read first. So, why is it that when we teach children to code, we often get them to write code before they can read it? This is the main rationale behind a three-stage approach to learning to code, known as 'use-modify-create'.

The idea behind this approach is to encourage children to 'use' an existing snippet of code and explore what it does, 'modify' (or tinker with) the code to change its behaviour and, once they understand how the program works, 'create' a new program of their own. This strategy complements the Papert-style approach of learning by exploring and tinkering.

Teaching tip

When moving to the 'create' phase, students should be encouraged to test, analyse and improve their programs regularly, just as they would do with any new project.

How it works

Use: Provide students with a snippet of working code. Give students time to run the program and figure out what the code is meant to do and how it works. Where appropriate, provide students with questions or prompts to aid with their investigations.

Modify: As the students become more comfortable with the program, encourage them to start changing it. For example, if the program is written in Scratch, the students could start by simply changing the sprite or by changing some of the variables. As the students' confidence begins to grow, they can start to make more complex changes to the code.

Create: Once the students are confident with how the program works, have them create their own program using what they have learned.

Hour of Code

'Give your students a "byte"-sized introduction to computer science with an hour of code.'

The Hour of Code started as a one-hour introduction to computer science, designed to demystify 'code' to show that anybody can learn the basics, and to broaden participation in the field of computer science.

Teaching tip

Don't worry if you're new to coding yourself. Hour of Code is geared towards beginners. It can be a great opportunity to learn along with your students – and in fact, that's part of the fun!

Hour of Code takes place each year during Computer Science Education Week (usually during the second or third week of December), to mark and celebrate the birth of computing pioneer Admiral Grace Murray Hopper (9 December 1906).

Why Hour of Code?

Every student should have the opportunity to learn computer science. It helps to nurture problem-solving skills, logic and creativity. By starting early, it may also encourage some students to take up computer science as a GCSE when it comes to their options.

How to participate in the Hour of Code

You can organise an Hour of Code event in your school at any time, not just during Computer Science Education Week. There is a handy guide to getting started on the official Hour of Code website (hourofcode.com/uk). Hour of Code can be delivered during normal lessons or as part of an extra-curricular club.

Where to start

Thankfully, you will find a plethora of resources available online dedicated to Hour of Code. Below are just a few of my favourites:

- Hour of Code: hourofcode.com/uk
- Code.org: code.org/hourofcode/overview
- Tynker: tynker.com/hour-of-code

#HourOfCode

Code bug

'To err is human but to really foul things up you need a computer.'

A great way to build resilience and reduce anxiety when teaching children how to code is to purposely introduce 'bugs' early on in the learning process.

Did you know that in 1947, a real bug (a moth to be exact) was found trapped in a computer's relay, causing it to short circuit! Although some believe that this is how the term 'bug' originated, evidence shows that the word 'bug' was being used in this context long before this. Thankfully, the bugs that your students are more likely to encounter will not be the six-legged variety but will, instead, be either logical errors (errors that allow the program to function but produce unintentional results) or syntax errors (errors, usually associated with spelling mistakes, that cause the program to stop working).

Start by sharing a simple program with some crucial lines of code deliberately omitted. I find that a good place to start is the turtle library in Scratch or Python (see Idea 87: Turtle power). Challenge students, in pairs, to identify the missing code. Set a timer for two minutes and ask students to discuss their answers with their partner. Take feedback from the class before revealing the solution.

Inform the students that computer programs often contain several lines of complex code and that, because of this, computer programs often contain mistakes. Tell the students that these mistakes are referred to as 'bugs'. Explain that an important part of programming is testing your program (also known as 'debugging') to remove all the bugs from your code.

Teaching tip

When providing pre-prepared examples, use the chosen language's commenting system to help the students to understand what the code is meant to do.

Taking it further

Put the students into pairs and hand out some pre-prepared samples of code containing both logical and syntax errors. Challenge students to predict what the code is meant to do before trying to fix the errors.

Bonus idea ★

Have students create their own programs containing deliberate errors for their partner to solve.

Code combat

'Put your students' coding skills to the test by pitting them against each other in code combat!'

Not to be confused with 'game-based learning' (see Idea 18), gamification is the process of introducing game-like elements into traditionally non-gaming contexts to make them fun and engaging. One activity that epitomises the gamification philosophy is 'code combat'.

Teaching tip

Some students may struggle with some elements of gamification, such as competing against their peers. One strategy to help to alleviate this is to introduce 'ghost mode'. In ghost mode, students try to beat their own high score rather than competing with others around them.

Taking it further

Other gamification strategies include elements such as gamifying grading, incentivising students with rewards and adding competitive elements such as leader boards.

Bonus idea ★

Have students create their own 'code combat' games to pit against their peers or to try to 'beat the teacher'!

Code combat (also referred to as code wars or code battles) is a programming strategy that encourages students to achieve 'code mastery' by completing a series of challenges, often against other opponents. Just like in a video game, in code combat students often receive rewards for successfully completing a challenge, such as unlocking achievements or gaining access to unique items (loot).

One form of code combat uses a simplified version of Parsons problems. Share some pre-prepared samples of code, each containing one or more deliberate errors (use a combination of logical and syntax errors). Split the class into small teams and have them compete against each other (or against a clock) to see who can spot and fix the deliberate errors fastest.

A variation of the previous example is called 'code Jenga®'. Start by preparing some working examples containing redundant lines of code (i.e. code that is not used by the main program but does not stop the program from functioning), for example, rogue variables. Students must then take it in turns to find and remove the redundant code, one line at a time (Jenga®-style), without causing the program to stop working. The losing team is the team that stops the program from working by removing an essential line of code.

Teaching with robots

'Programming can often be difficult for students to grasp. Robots can provide a simpler, more tangible introduction to programming.'

Experience tells us that hands-on learning, such as programming robots, empowers students to learn actively by challenging them to solve 'real-world' problems rather than contrived scenarios.

Ever since Seymour Papert introduced the programming language LOGO, best known for its implementation of turtle graphics and 'floor turtle' (an early programmable floor robot) in the late 1960s, there has been a growing interest in using robots to help teach computer science education in schools.

Teaching tip

Get the students to play with the robots first so that they understand the capabilities and limitations of the robots before programming them!

When students program physical robots, they are able to see the immediate impact of their code and are more likely to identify errors in their instructions. The following are examples of robots that are particularly suited for classroom use:

Sphero

Sphero offers a range of programmable robots, ranging from the budget-friendly Sphero Mini to the 'all-terrain' programmable RVR robot. Each robot comes with a dedicated app and collection of suggested lesson ideas.

Tello Edu drone

Tello is a programmable mini drone. Its small form factor and great durability make the Tello drone perfect for classroom use. Tello can be programmed using the dedicated app or via Apple's Swift Playgrounds.

LEGO® EV3

The LEGO® EV3 is a programmable robotics kit from the creators of LEGO®. The robot can be programmed using blocks (via the dedicated app) or with MicroPython.

Bonus idea ★

Challenge students to adapt/modify their robot to meet a specific need or purpose, e.g. building an arm to support a pen/paintbrush.

Computing
strategies

Part 2

Take your screwdrivers to work

'Miss, am I supposed to have this many screws left over?'

Possibly one of the most popular — and probably the most hands-on — topics in computer science theory is how computers work. I find that this is a great excuse to grab some old computers and a set of screwdrivers and take the old computers apart.

Teaching tip

Encourage the students to photograph the inside of the PC before taking it apart and use this as a reference guide for putting it back together!

Taking it further

For a little extra competition when playing 'You Say We Pay', you can also split the class into two and take it in turns to see which team can get the most correct answers.

Put the students into groups of four or five and give each group a set of screwdrivers and an old PC. Challenge the students to take the PC apart, making a note of where each component goes, and then put it back together again.

As the students take the computer apart, you can get them to label or photograph each component and write a brief description. These can then be used to create an interactive wall display (see Idea 19: Using QR codes) or uploaded to a VLE/Wiki to form part of a revision resource.

If you are feeling really brave, you could challenge your students to put the computers back together and switch them on to see whether they will boot up!

To consolidate the learning, I recommend finishing off the lesson by playing a game of 'You Say We Pay'! If you have never played the game before, this is a game borrowed from *Richard and Judy*. The aim of the game is for one student, blindfolded or with back turned to the whiteboard, to guess which computer components are being displayed using only descriptions given from the class (the students describing each component are not allowed to say the component's name or use words that rhyme, e.g. 'sounds like ...').

DART your students

'I'm sure you're not allowed to dart us, Sir!'

Don't worry, it's not as bad as it sounds! DART (directed activity related to text) is a strategy designed to improve students' reading comprehension. It focuses on the strategies of skimming, scanning and gap-fill.

DART activities are great for introducing a new topic, consolidating learning or assessing students' understanding, and can be used with individuals, small groups or pairs of students. A number of DART activities, such as prediction, sequencing and reconstruction, naturally lend themselves to the teaching of computer science. The most common types are:

Gap-fill: These activities require the student to understand the context of a given piece of text in order to correctly identify the missing words or phrases. A passage is shared with the students, with key words or information missing. The students are then challenged to fill in the missing words, phrases or sentences as they read.

Prediction: In this type of activity, students are required to analyse a piece of given text and predict what happens next. The key here is for students not to guess what happens next, but to evaluate the information available and support their predictions with evidence/logical reasoning.

Sequencing: These types of activity require students to reorganise a jumbled piece of text into a logical order/correct sequence.

Grouping: Students are required to group segments of text according to categories.

Reconstruction: Students are challenged to reconstruct a piece of given text in the form of a diagram, table, flow chart or sketch.

Teaching tip

When using gap-fill exercises, don't give students the first letter of the missing word, as this can reduce the activity to a low-level exercise. Gap-fill exercises can be easily differentiated by either increasing or decreasing the number of missing words, changing the complexity of the missing words or giving students a list of possible words to choose from.

Contextualise learning

'Sir, what's a floppy disk?'

By making computing relevant and providing a 'real-life' context, you can create meaningful learning experiences for your students!

Teaching tip

Using examples from popular culture is a great way to make learning relevant. For example, when teaching binary representation of sound and images, I often use trending (or viral) themes – Baby shark doo doo doo doo doo...

The most common questions you will get asked by students when undertaking a new topic or subject are:

- Why are we doing this?
- Will this help me with my exam?
- When will I ever use this?
- Will this help me get a job?

In other words, how is it relevant?

Contextualisation is not about changing the learning outcomes or objectives. It's about modifying the learning materials so that they have relevance to the students.

To make computer science relevant, when planning or delivering a new computing activity, ask yourself the following questions:

Personal
- Does this relate to students' aspirations?
- Can it be related to students' common interests?

Professional
- Can it help students to understand how computing is relevant when making future career choices?
- Does it involve skills that can be used in the workplace?

Social
- Can it be linked to popular culture?
- Does it relate to a recent newsworthy event?

Go unplugged

'Computer science is no more about computers than astronomy is about telescopes.' (Often attributed to Edsger Dijkstra)

One thing that frustrates many computing teachers is the amount of valuable time wasted due to technical issues. One way I have found to make better use of classroom time is to 'go unplugged'!

The 'unplugged' style of teaching refers to the act of teaching areas of the computing curriculum without the need for computers.

While the idea of teaching computing without computers may seem a little strange at first, I can honestly say that some of my best lessons have been completely away from a computer screen. One example that epitomises the unplugged approach is the 'Jam Sandwich Algorithm' devised by Phil Bagge (code-it. co.uk). In this exercise, pupils are asked to create an algorithm from set commands to program their teacher (the 'sandwich bot') to make a jam sandwich.

Pupils must write a set of working instructions, using commands such as 'Pick up' and 'Put down', which their teacher has to follow precisely to make a jam sandwich. The key to success is for the teacher to be as pedantic as possible (i.e. to follow the children's instructions *exactly*). For example, if a child writes the instruction 'Spread the jam', the teacher could respond by spreading some jam on the table or using their fingers – obviously, the messier and sillier, the better! By being pedantic, this should hopefully encourage the children to refine their instructions to try to 'beat the teacher'. At the end of the activity, the teacher can relate this to programming and can use the lessons learned to explore the importance of precise instructions when writing code.

Teaching tip

Going unplugged is not a panacea, nor is it a one-size-fits-all strategy! Some students will find unplugged concepts a little too abstract, while others will not care for the kinaesthetic approach. As with any new strategy, it is always a good idea to 'mix and match' different approaches.

Socratic debate

'The aim of an argument or discussion should not be victory, but progress.' (Joseph Joubert)

One approach that I have used to teach computing theory with great success is Socratic debate. Socratic debates are great for tackling emotive and challenging topics such as social, ethical and legal issues surrounding the use of computers.

Unlike a conventional debate, in a Socratic debate, the students help each other to explore ideas and arrive at an answer by asking and answering questions. The students are responsible for facilitating their own group discussion, while also practising listening and questioning skills.

Split the class into two teams and introduce the main topic. After some initial research, instruct the teams to compile their best arguments and choose their spokespersons, before entering the 'Socratic circle'. Prior to the discussion, prepare some questions for those students who are not leading the discussion, such as, 'Who gave the most persuasive argument – boys or girls?' or 'Who used quotes in their arguments?' and ask students to write down examples. This will ensure that everyone is involved during the debate.

Let the students decide who will lead the discussion and explain the rules. Arrange the seats into two circles (inner and outer) – the inner circle should have fewer seats. Direct the students to their designated seats (inner circle: discussion group; outer circle: listening group). Give students in the outer circle one of the pre-prepared 'focus cards' with a particular task to concentrate on.

Start the discussion with an opening question or statement and then let the students dictate the pace themselves.

Teaching tip

As with any form of debate, it is always good to start with a set of ground rules:

- Respect each other's opinions.
- One voice at a time.
- Listen carefully to everyone's argument.
- Support your arguments with evidence.
- If you don't understand something, ask!
- Try to reach an agreement.

Once these rules are understood, you should try only to become involved when it is time to wrap up or if the discussion starts to lag by introducing a new question.

Taking it further

Finish the discussion by asking the students in the outer circle to reveal their question or mission to the rest of the class and to respond with their observations.

Peer instruction

'One approach to teaching difficult concepts that students often misunderstand is peer instruction.'

Peer instruction is a technique pioneered by Eric Mazur, Professor of Physics and Applied Physics at Harvard. It is closely associated with the flipped classroom approach (see Idea 22).

Peer instruction relies heavily on carefully selected questions, often based around some pre-instruction material (notes, video, etc). Multiple-choice questions (MCQs) are perfect for this type of scenario, as they contain answers known as distractors (plausible wrong answers), which can reflect the students' common misconceptions.

How it works

- Pick a topic that students often find difficult or commonly misunderstand.
- Set some preparatory work for students to complete before the session.
- Start the lesson by posing a pre-prepared MCQ. Give the students limited time to vote on the answer using voting cards, clickers, etc.
- Put the students into small groups and have them discuss the question before agreeing on one answer.
- Display the question again, now asking the students to respond with their agreed answer.
- Finish by displaying the correct answer and discussing the common misconceptions.

Example question
Consider the following Python code:
```
a = 20
b = 10
a = b
```
What are the values of a and b?
1) a = 10, b = 10; 2) a = 20, b = 20; 3) a = 30, b = 10; 4) a = 10, b = 20

Teaching tip

Walk around the classroom during peer discussions and listen out for any common misconceptions. You can then explore these as part of a plenary or use them as distractors in future MCQs.

Bonus idea

Show students the change between the first and second attempt, so that they can see the difference that peer instruction made.

Game-based learning

'Miss, did you say that we're going to be playing Minecraft?'

Not to be confused with gamification (see Idea 10), game-based learning (GBL) is the process of using games to achieve a defined set of learning outcomes. One game that I use to help teach computing is Minecraft.

Teaching tip

Before moving to coding in Minecraft, it is recommended that students explore the game first in order to get used to the controls and game mechanics.

Taking it further

In Minecraft: Education Edition, there is also a programmable robot (called Agent), which you can program much like a floor robot but in Minecraft!

Bonus idea ★

Have students create pixel art (see Idea 92: Art attack) by placing blocks using code.

What is Minecraft?

Minecraft is a sandbox game where players have to build structures using 2 m³ blocks.

Using Minecraft to teach Boolean logic

Computer memory uses many small transistors and capacitors to store data. A transistor is a tiny switch that is activated by the electronic signals that it receives. The digits 1 and 0 used in binary reflect the on and off states of a transistor. These transistors can be wired together to make a circuit that performs simple, logical calculations. These simple circuits are called logic gates.

In Minecraft, there is a special type of block called redstone. Because redstone has two states (on or off), it can be used to create simple logic gates. A quick online search will unearth several tutorials showing you how to create simple AND, OR and NOT gates in Minecraft. These can be used as a basis to create more complex logic circuits.

Using Minecraft to teach coding

Minecraft: Education Edition and Minecraft Pi (Raspberry Pi Edition) allow you to code in Minecraft. While Minecraft Pi focuses mainly on Python, Minecraft: Education Edition allows you to code using a combination of Python, JavaScript and MakeCode (block-based programming language).

Using QR codes

'As mobile learning becomes more prevalent, we must find effective ways to leverage the power of mobile technologies in the classroom.'

A QR code (quick response code) is a machine-readable code made up of black and white squares, which, when scanned by a web-enabled device, can access a range of online materials. Thanks to a plethora of free apps and online tools, creating your own multimedia-rich QR experiences has never been easier.

How it works

1 Install and load your preferred QR-creation tool (see examples below).
2 Paste in the URL of the content that you wish to trigger from your QR code (this could be a website, YouTube video, podcast, OneNote or pretty much anything with a web address).
3 Print out the automatically generated QR code.
4 Install and run your preferred QR reader.
5 Point your device's camera at your QR code.

What you need

- a web-enabled device with built-in camera (e.g. tablet, netbook or smartphone)
- a QR-creation tool, such as Qrafter (iOS), QR Code for Windows 10, Barcode Generator (Android) or QR Stuff.com (web)
- a QR reader, such as QR Reader (Windows 10), QR Code Reader (iOS) or QR Code Reader from Kaywa (Android). Note: Some Android and iOS devices already have the ability to read QR codes built in.

Suggested applications

- Create an interactive wall display – for example, showing the inside workings of a computer.
- Create a QR treasure hunt in which students have to collect information about hardware components from codes strategically hidden on related devices.

Teaching tip

QR codes are great for sharing long and complex URLs such as those shared by online classroom-management tools, such as Google Classroom and Office 365.

Taking it further

You could also create a QR timeline – for example, a timeline of influential computer scientists.

Escape rooms

'Sir, can I get out now?'

Escape rooms are increasing in popularity, so it was only a matter of time before the idea made its way into the classroom.

Teaching tip

Don't worry if students fail to unlock all the padlocks. It's not about beating the game; it's about developing problem-solving and critical thinking skills.

The 'escape room' model sees players willingly locked in a room and, by searching for clues and completing a series of challenges, they race against the clock to 'break out'! Obviously, the idea of locking children in a room and hoping that they will break out is somewhat frowned upon. Thankfully, there is a more child-friendly version called 'BreakoutEdu'!

What is BreakoutEdu?

BreakoutEdu is an off-shoot of the popular 'escape room' game, which sees students solve puzzles in order to open physical locks. Often, several locks of differing types (numeric, alpha-numeric, directional, etc.) are connected to one box with the aid of a multi-hasp to make things more challenging.

Traditionally, break-out games require students to solve clues in order to open physical padlocks. However, if you don't want to go down the route of purchasing numerous locks, there are a number of 'digital' alternatives, such as password-protected files or pages, for example, in OneNote.

Not only are escape rooms fun and engaging, but they also help to build resilience as well as promoting problem-solving and critical thinking — all of which are key skills attributed to the studying of computer science.

Example (binary break-out)

What you will need:

- lockable container
- multi-lock hasp
- five-letter combo lock
- four-digit combo lock
- three-digit combo lock
- ASCII to binary table
- paper/pencils.

Prior to the lesson, prepare some binary puzzles for the students to solve and set each of the padlocks to match the corresponding solutions. (Top tip: Make sure that you keep a note of all passwords and combinations!) For example:

1 Five-letter combo lock:
   0100 0011 | 0100 0001 | 0101 0100 |
   0100 0011 | 0100 1000
   Answer: CATCH (ASCII)

2 Four-digit combo lock:
   0001 | 0101 | 1001 | 1000
   Answer: 1598

3 Three-digit combo lock:

	0	1	1	0
+	0	0	0	1

	0	0	1	1
+	0	0	1	0

	0	0	0	1
+	1	0	0	0

   Answer: 759

Before the lesson starts, place a message inside a lockable container – for example, 'We broke out!' Split the class into teams of four and hand out the puzzle worksheets. Set a timer for 20 minutes and challenge the students to break open the locks before the time runs out!

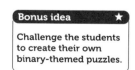

Bonus idea ★

Challenge the students to create their own binary-themed puzzles.

#BreakoutEdu

Blogs and wikis

'Foster collaboration and support learning beyond the limits of the classroom!'

Blogs (or web logs) and wikis are increasingly being used in education by teachers and students. They can provide a communication tool that teachers can use with students to develop writing, share ideas and reflect on work being undertaken in the classroom. Blogs and wikis also provide a perfect platform for creating teacher-made or student-generated classroom and revision resources!

Teaching tip

Collaborating in the same workspace can provide a challenge for some students. One solution to this problem is to place the students into small groups and provide each group with a sub-topic or challenge. For example, if exploring different types of memory, one group could focus on cache memory while another focuses on virtual memory, etc.

Being web-based, a blog or wiki can help to provide an immersive learning experience for your students. Not only that, but when the focus is on the students creating their own class blogs or wikis, it can also help to personalise learning and place ownership of the learning firmly in the hands of the students.

Thanks to a plethora of free online tools, such as Weebly, Wix and PB Works, as well as features built into classroom-management systems such as Google Classroom, etc., teachers and students can easily create secure blogs or classroom wikis, with little or no prior knowledge of web design!

Examples:

- Have students create a blog or wiki for exam revision.
- Create a blog or wiki to introduce a new topic (see Idea 22: Flipped learning).
- Use a blog or wiki to identify key computing terminology or share the definitions of command words used in exams, etc.
- Have students use a blog or wiki to manage a project.

Flipped learning

'Make better use of classroom time by flipping your classroom!'

Flipped learning essentially reverses the traditional way of teaching, so what is normally done as homework is carried out during lesson time while what is usually done during lesson time, such as instruction and exploring theory, is carried out prior to the lesson as homework. The main benefit of this model is that the students have more time to practise their new skills.

How it works

- Choose a topic to flip, such as binary addition.
- Create, or source from the internet, some instructional or reference material to introduce your new topic – for example, how to add two 4-bit binary numbers.
- Publish the resources online via the school's VLE, a blog post, wiki or classroom-management system.
- Instruct your students to review the resources prior to the next lesson as homework. Inform the students that they will be tested on the content.
- Start the lesson with a short test. This will help not only to reinforce the key learning but will also provide an opportunity to address any misunderstandings.
- Use the lesson to explore the topic in more detail or have the students practise what they have learned with some practical examples.

Tools for facilitating flipped learning

- **Video tutorials:** Otherwise known as vodcasting, the most common way to flip your classroom is to use teacher-created videos that students can view outside of the classroom.
- **Blogs and wikis:** Blogs and wikis are the perfect platform for sharing multimedia-rich content suitable for flipped learning.

Teaching tip

Prepare your students! This style of teaching and learning will be as new to them as it is to you. Make sure that you share your expectations with them from the outset and ensure that they understand the reasons for the change!

Taking it further

Podcasts are an ideal companion for the flipped classroom as they are compatible with a wide range of portable devices and can be accessed pretty much anytime, anywhere!

Guided discovery

'Sir, did you know it could do that?'

Guided discovery, also known as guided exploration, is an inductive approach to teaching and learning where students take an active role in discovering knowledge and developing understanding for themselves.

Teaching tip

To help to support the discovery phase, use strategies such as C3B4ME and SNOT (Self, Neighbour, Other, Teacher). This will encourage the students to seek help from their peers before getting help from the teacher.

Taking it further

Once students have mastered the commands, have them explore two or more commands on their own.

Guided discovery encourages independence and can make learning more memorable but, like any new strategy, it is not without its pitfalls. To be successful, the teacher must select tasks that are appropriate for the level for the students and structure the lesson so that all learners remain within their 'zone of proximal development', i.e. between what they can do without help and what they can achieve with guidance and scaffolding from the teacher.

Guided discovery lends itself well to activities that involve students having to learn a new skill or explore new features in a piece of software, such as Scratch or Photoshop.

How it works

Start by providing two or three features from your chosen application that the students must explore – have an idea in mind before the lesson of what you want the students to learn. For example, if exploring Scratch, the focus could be on particular blocks such as 'Motion' or 'Events' or, if using Photoshop, the focus could be on different selection tools or filters. Next, rather than demonstrating what the features do, have the students draw on their existing knowledge of the application to figure out what the commands do by themselves. Have some carefully selected pre-prepared questions ready to help students focus on the key learning objectives and also to address any misconceptions or misunderstandings.

ICT and
digital literacy

Part 3

Fake news

'Miss, dehydrated water must be real because there's a "buy it now" button!'

In a digital world riddled with 'fake news' stories, students need to be aware of the potential pitfalls when consuming news, particularly when using online sources.

Teaching tip

When deciding whether each website is 'real' or 'fake', encourage students to use the five Ws:

- Where is the article located?
- What information is the article providing?
- When was the article created/updated?
- Why would you use the article as a source of information?
- Who is the source of the information?

Start by asking the students to explain what they think is meant by the term 'fake news'. Draw out answers such as 'news or stories on the internet that are not true' and 'news or stories designed to make people believe things that are made up', etc.

Ask the students if they check whether a story is true before they share it with their friends. Explain to pupils that fake images are often used to help corroborate a story and make it appear more believable.

Inform the students that they will be assuming the role of internet detectives whose job is to spot the fakes from a selection of websites. Put the students into pairs and share the following list of websites. Instruct the students to visit each website on the list below and decide which sites are 'fake' or 'real' and explain why.

Websites:

- https://zapatopi.net/treeoctopus – Save the Tree Octopus (fake)
- www.thedogisland.com – Dog Island (fake)
- www.allaboutexplorers.com/explorers/drake – All About Explorers (fake)
- https://savingtherennets.weebly.com – Save the Rennets (fake)
- http://www.ripleys.com – Ripley's Believe It or Not (real)

Discuss the answers with the students and ask them to justify their decisions.

Copy cat

'Sir, that's my work, not Sam's!'

Our students are regularly taught about their 'digital footprint' and the dangers of being online, and rightfully so, but one area of digital literacy that I find is often overlooked is copyright and Creative Commons.

As well as being taught how to stay safe online, students should also know about copyright, public domain, fair use and Creative Commons.

Prior to the lesson, choose some samples of students' work and deliberately change the authors' names. As the students enter the classroom, have the students' altered work on show and ask them to discuss, with a partner, what is wrong with the work. Draw out answers such as, 'Work has the wrong name attached', 'Work has been copied' and 'Work has been stolen', etc. Ask the students how they feel about their work being credited to someone else. Stimulate discussion by asking questions such as, 'What is wrong with the images?' and 'Why does it matter if someone else is credited with their work?' Select pairs at random to explain how they felt when they saw someone else's name on their work.

Inform the students that the work they make belongs to them. Explain that, just like the work that the students had created, the images we find online belong to someone and we need the authors' permission to use them!

Explain that, to make it easier for people to get permission to use other people's work, a system was introduced called 'Creative Commons' licences. Inform the students that Creative Commons licences allow people to share their work freely in return for recognition of their work (also known as attribution).

Teaching tip

Share with students the four most common Creative Commons symbols (BY, NC, ND and SA) and explain what each symbol means: https://creativecommons.org/licenses.

Taking it further

Demonstrate how to use the 'usage rights' tool in Google Images and/or 'license' tool in Bing to search for free-to-use/Creative Commons images and challenge the students to find some free-to-use images for a topic of their choice.

Bonus idea

Model how to attribute other people's work and challenge students to attribute the images that they have found.

Mario Kart™ spreadsheets

'Sir, did you actually say that we are going to be playing Mario Kart™?'

Game-based learning (GBL) is the process of using games to achieve a defined set of learning outcomes. Games that generate data, e.g. Kinect Sports and Mario Kart™, are great for teaching maths and statistics. Games that tell a story are great for developing creative writing. Puzzle games can develop problem-solving, and physics-based games, such as Angry Birds, can be used to explain velocity and momentum.

Teaching tip

Use a random name selector or draw names from a hat to choose who goes first, or use multi-player or online games to allow more than one student to play at the same time.

Taking it further

Challenge students to create graphs from their data or create a podium, using a column chart, showing who came first, second and third.

One game that I have used to teach spreadsheets to great effect is Mario Kart™. Why Mario Kart™? In my experience, students respond better and engage more when using 'authentic' data that they have collected/generated themselves, such as from healthy competition, as opposed to using contrived examples that have no context or relevance to the students.

In order to practise spreadsheet skills, students take it in turns to complete laps around a course in Mario Kart™. The students then compile the raw data generated by the class and input this into a suitable spreadsheet. The students then use basic and advanced skills to improve the look and functionality of their spreadsheet. Note: You don't have to use Mario Kart™! You can use any game that generates scores or lap times.

Inform students that they are going to take it in turns to complete a time trial in Mario Kart™ (or game of your choosing) and record their track times in a shared spreadsheet. Explain that while each player records their fastest lap around the course, the rest of the class must create a spreadsheet to collate/organise the data into fastest time, average time and leader board. Have students start building their spreadsheet model while each player takes it in turns to complete a time trial circuit in Mario Kart™.

Fakebook

'Sir, are you trying to catfish us?'

One way to teach children about the importance of keeping personal data secure online is to have them take on the role of a cyber-criminal!

Prior to the lesson, create a fake online profile using Word or Publisher and include the following information:

1. A fake name (for example, Chloe Smith);
2. profile picture; 3. birthday (e.g. 12 May);
4. a dated post wishing her a happy 18th birthday; 5. hobbies and interests;
6. a post mentioning her pet's name; 7. a post mentioning her address; 8. a picture of her school's logo/crest.

Next, create a password-protected file or section in OneNote (I suggest using her pet's name followed by her year of birth, e.g. Boris2002) containing the following message: 'Congratulations, you have successfully recovered Chloe's password! Chloe has just moved to a new school. Can you plan her route from home?' (Students should be able to upload the school logo/crest to a Bing/Google image search to find the location of the school.)

Inform the students that Chloe has forgotten her password but, as her profile is open for anyone to see, she has asked you to help her search for clues on her profile to recover her password. Explain that once the students have recovered the password, they can use it to unlock the password-protected page and reveal the next challenge. At the end of the challenge, explain to the students that they weren't actually trying to help Chloe, but instead were taking on the role of a cyber-criminal! Discuss with the students how easy it was to piece together all of Chloe's personal data.

Teaching tip

Classroom tools (www.classtools.net/FB/home-page) provide a free handy tool for creating Facebook-like profile pages.

Taking it further

Have students discuss the importance of privacy settings when using social media.

Bonus idea ★

Challenge students to think of a new password for Chloe. Explain that the password needs to be easy for her to remember but difficult for others to crack!

Database detectives

'Miss, who is Sherlock Holmes?'

OK, so students are more likely to have heard of Rastamouse than Sherlock Holmes, but whether you're a fan of Miss Marple or your favourite sleuth is Tintin, everyone loves a good mystery!

Taking it further

Challenge students to improve their queries by including at least one Boolean operator (AND/OR/NOT) and one wildcard (*).

One way that I have found to make the teaching of database skills more interesting is to use them to solve a mystery!

What you will need:

1 a scenario in which an item was stolen or someone was murdered
2 a database of suspects with, as a minimum, the following fields: name, age, gender, height, hair colour, distinguishing feature, blood group
3 witness statement(s) and list of evidence.

Example: The Case of the Stolen Poodle

Witness 1: Lord Byron, age 61, height 1.64 m
Witness 2: Lady Byron, age 59, height 1.60 m

Witness statement 1: We were returning from the cinema and, as we pulled onto the driveway, the house alarm was ringing. I jumped out of the car and investigated. A man, a little shorter than me, ran past carrying a large bag.
Witness statement 2: As the person was running past me, I managed to trip them. The person fell to the floor but managed to escape.
Evidence: Blood sample (group A), broken spectacles.

Bonus idea ★

Challenge students to create their own scenario using the database of suspects.

Challenge students to compile a list of suspects by using a combination of queries and database filters. For example (SQL):
SELECT * FROM Suspects
WHERE Gender='Male'
AND Height<1.64;

Did you meme it?

'Use popular culture as a conversation starter or to contextualise learning!'

Using examples from popular culture can help to contextualise learning and provide a stimulus when teaching computing concepts. A perfect example is the use of memes to explore image manipulation and e-safety themes.

Start by asking the students to explain what a meme is. Draw out answers, such as 'a funny picture or video to which someone has added text'. Ask students to discuss memes that they have seen or created themselves.

Share some example memes and discuss with the class the key features. For example:

- layout (How have the images and text been laid out? Why might that be?)
- text (What font types, sizes and colours have been used? What effects have been used?)
- images (How does the image relate to the message on the meme?).

Model how to create a meme using your favourite image-editing software (or presentation tool). Challenge the students to create their own memes on a suitably chosen/ agreed topic. At this point, remind students that memes often have a hint of humour, and encourage them to consider this when creating their memes.

Finish the lesson by asking for volunteers to share their memes with the rest of the class. Use questioning to stimulate discussion. For example: What images did they use? What influenced their image choice? What fonts and colours did they use? What problems did they encounter when creating their memes and how did they solve them? Does the meme fulfil its intended purpose?

Teaching tip

Encourage students to THINK before sharing memes, or any other form of online media!

T = is it true?
H = is it helpful?
I = is it inspiring?
N = is it necessary?
K = is it kind?

Taking it further

Ask more confident pupils to demonstrate to the rest of the class some of the skills and techniques that they used to create their meme.

Videography

'When I grow up, I want to be a YouTuber!'

There was a time when, if I asked students what they would like to do when they left school, the most likely answer would have been footballer, reality TV star or, occasionally, teacher! Nowadays, I tend to find that a lot of students want to be a YouTuber!

Teaching tip

Not even the professionals record their videos in one take, so don't expect your students to. Have them split their video into smaller chunks (or chapters) or record the voice-overs during post production.

Bonus idea ★

Have students create a video intro or channel art for their YouTube video.

Thankfully, you don't need to be an expert in Adobe Premier to create professional-looking YouTube videos! Thanks to tools such as iMovie (Mac/iOS), Photos (Windows) and tools readily available on most modern smartphones, creating videos for YouTube has never been easier!

Challenge students to create their own YouTube-style instructional videos to demonstrate how to apply an effect in Photoshop (see Idea 100: Colour splash), build a simple structure in Minecraft (see Idea 18: Game-based learning) or explain how to add two binary numbers (in preparation for an exam), for example.

Before creating their videos, have the students create a storyboard and draft a script. This will not only provide a great opportunity to incorporate literacy, by having the students use imperative verbs (flip, rotate, attach, etc.) and time connectives (firstly, eventually, finally, etc.), but will also help to reinforce the relationship between step-by-step instructions and algorithms.

Infographics

'Seventy-three point six per cent of all statistics are made up!'

In today's digital age, being able to communicate information in a clear, simple and impactful way is essential! Infographics are a great educational tool that not only helps students to convey their message but also helps them to engage with data.

Start by choosing an area to investigate – something relatable but also quantifiable, such as a survey on students' mobile phone habits. Next, have the students create a poll and collect information on their chosen topic.

Put the students into pairs and share some example infographics (good.is/infographics is a great source for this). Have the students identify and list all of the key features. After a few minutes have elapsed, have the pairs swap places with their neighbours and add to each others' lists. Ask for volunteers to list some of the key features. Draw out answers such as 'very little text', 'lots of images', 'pictograms, charts and graphs', 'few colours', etc.

Demonstrate on the board various ways to represent the same data and discuss, as a class, which has the most impact and why.

Finally, challenge the students to design an infographic based on the results of their poll. Inform the students that they can use any tools that they wish to create their infographic, but they should consider the following design rules:

- Use catchy titles, e.g. 'Did you know?'
- Use lots of visuals.
- List all sources.
- Stick to two or three colours.
- Use charts instead of tables.

Teaching tip

To give you an example, the statistic that 90 per cent of students own a smartphone could be represented as follows:

- pie chart or bar chart (showing a 90/10 split)
- pictogram (for example, nine coloured smartphone icons and one greyed-out smartphone icon)
- smartphone battery icon indicating 90 per cent
- table or plain text.

Teaching tip

You don't need expensive design tools to create impactful infographics! Presentation tools such as Microsoft PowerPoint are perfect for this scenario.

Taking it further

Explain the difference between 'vector' and 'bitmap' images and have the students explain which is most appropriate for their infographic.

Dragons' Den

'Bring out the entrepreneur in your students with a *Dragons' Den*-style challenge!'

Dragons' Den is a popular TV show in which entrepreneurs pitch their business ideas to a panel of venture capitalists in the hope of securing an investment.

Teaching tip

To add some authenticity to the challenge, have the students pitch their idea to a panel of judges ('Dragons'). This panel can be made up entirely – or by a combination – of other teachers, sixth formers or members of the local business community.

Start by telling the students that they have been challenged to create an app or device to help address an everyday problem. Inform the students that they will be pitching their idea to a panel of judges (or 'Dragons'), who will decide whether they want to invest in their idea.

Put the students into small groups and have them compile a list of problems that they may have encountered in their daily lives or issues that they might be aware of. These could be global issues, such as climate change or global waste, or something that affects the students themselves or their community, such as graffiti in their local park or litter in the school playground. Next, have them decide on one that they are passionate about!

Introduce the 'root cause tree' to assist them in getting to the root of their problem. Students can either draw their own trees or use a template, sourced from the internet. First, instruct the students to write the problem that they have identified into the trunk of the tree. Next, in the five main roots of the tree, have the students write down the five main reasons why they believe the problem occurs. Once the students have identified the five root causes, have them choose one that they would like to solve using technology.

Bonus idea ★

Students could make a prototype of their idea using physical components, e.g. with a micro:bit, or using app-creation software such as App Inventor.

#DragonsDen

Once the students have agreed on a problem, challenge them to design an inventive solution (app or device) and pitch their idea to the class.

Wayback Machine

'Everything you post online stays online forever!'

I came across this idea at a TeachMeet and thought it a wonderful way to teach students about their digital footprint.

Start by showing a picture of a footprint in the sand. Ask the students to explain what is meant by the term 'digital footprint'. Draw out answers such as 'your online history' and 'a trail that people leave behind online'. Inform the students that a digital footprint is a trail that you leave behind whenever you do something online, whether it is a comment on Facebook, a tweet or an image posted to Instagram. Explain that your digital footprint is a bit like a footprint that you leave in the sand, only these footprints will not wash away.

Explain to the students that anything you post online stays online forever. To illustrate this, direct students to the Wayback Machine (web. archive.org). Wayback Machine is a digital archive of the World Wide Web. It allows you to go 'back in time' and see what websites looked like in the past. Instruct the students to search for a suitable website, for example, bbc.co.uk, and choose a date before they were born. By choosing a date before they were born, I find that students are genuinely shocked and amazed that their digital content may still be accessible many years in the future!

> **Taking it further**
>
> Share the video 'Orange Digital Dirt' (www.youtube.com/watch?v=JJfw3xt4emY). Have the students discuss whether it is right for employees or universities to view your digital footprint when you're making an application and what can be done to protect your online profile.

> **Bonus idea** ★
>
> Challenge the students to create an advert or poster to encourage others to 'think before they post'.

Computing activities

Part 4

What a waste!

'Empower your students to make a positive impact on the environment!'

Electronic waste (or e-waste) is fast becoming a towering problem. The 50 million tonnes of e-waste generated every year is estimated to more than double by 2050. Our students have an important role in helping to reduce the amount of e-waste that we create.

Teaching tip

Students could share their ideas in the form of an infographic, poster, presentation or video.

Taking it further

Have the students create a guide for consumers on how to discard old electronic devices safely and securely.

Bonus idea ★

Launch a school-wide campaign (or have the class deliver an assembly) to educate others about the effects of e-waste and what can be done to tackle the problem.

Introduce the lesson by asking the students whether they can think of ways in which the increased use of technology impacts on the environment. Ask the students what they think the term 'e-waste' means. Draw out answers such as 'electronic waste' or 'waste generated by electronic devices that are thrown away and sent to landfill', etc.

Explain to the students that metals and plastics are used to manufacture computer components, while energy is consumed in making and using them. Inform them that some computer components contain toxic materials, such as lead, that are harmful to the environment and some are difficult to recycle.

Put the students into small groups and ask them to research the effects of e-waste on the environment and explore strategies for reducing the amount of e-waste that we create. Have the students share their findings in a shared document via OneNote or Padlet, for example.

Challenge the students in their groups to create a list of innovative ways to reduce e-waste. For example, manufacturers could use recycled materials, offer trade-in options to encourage consumers to trade in an old device in return for money off a new one, or make devices upgradable to extend their life. Consumers could reduce their e-waste by recycling old electronic devices or donating them to charity.

Role reversal

'Never be afraid to let your students teach you!'

If there is one thing that I have learned from being a teacher, it is: never be afraid to learn from your students!

Put the students into pairs and ask them to list all the different types of software that they can think of. After a few minutes, ask the students to swap their list with the pair next to them and add anything that they think is missing from their neighbours' list. After reviewing the students' suggestions, explain that software can be grouped into one of three categories:

Teaching tip

You can ask the students to swap places as many times as you like. By the end of the activity, the students should have a wide-ranging list of different types of software.

- **Application software:** software designed to allow users to perform specific tasks, such as word-processing, browsing the web, image editing, etc.
- **Operating system:** responsible for managing hardware and software resources, such as user interface, memory management and security.
- **Utility software:** programs that add functionality or perform maintenance tasks to a computer such as virus/malware protection, disk management, etc.

Inform the students that they are going to take on the role of the teacher. Tell them that each group will be given a different type of software to research and must present their findings to the class. How they present their findings is totally up to them. Put the students into small groups and give each group a challenge card with a topic to research and a set of tasks:

- Explain the purpose of your software.
- Describe how/when you would use it.
- List/name examples of your software.
- Identify the main features (video/ screenshots).

Storage Top Trumps®

'A great way to engage students in a subject or topic is to get them to create a game based on that topic.'

It is well documented how using games in a classroom context can facilitate collaborative learning, promote problem-solving and stimulate an engaging learning environment. One game that I have used to great effect is the popular card game Top Trumps®!

Teaching tip

The game works best with three teams; however, if you have more than three teams, you could play more than one round, with the winner of each round playing against each other in the final.

To begin with, students will need to be told various aspects of what to look for when choosing a secondary storage medium and what is expected of them in terms of creating the Top Trumps® cards. To provide some context, I recommend starting by explaining some of the key things to consider, namely, cost, capacity, speed of access, portability, durability, reliability, etc.

After a brief discussion about each of the key features and how they might be compared, decide as a class which features (or categories) to include on each card. This is important, especially if you plan for the students to play the game, as the students must have the same features on each of their respective cards.

Finally, challenge the students to create their own Top Trumps® cards by researching the features of different storage devices. I find that a great place to start is BBC Bitesize (bbc.co.uk/bitesize/guides/z67j2nb/revision/3). Here you will find a comparison table for each of the key features. (Note: The students can use a pre-built template, perhaps in Word, or an online Top Trumps® card-creator to create their cards.) Students must also include an image for each storage type.

How to play the game

1 Divide the class into three teams. Ask each team to designate a leader (this is the person who will turn over each of their pre-printed cards).

2 Instruct each team to shuffle their cards and place them face down on the table.

3 Ask the players to look at their top card but tell them not to show their card to the opposing teams.

4 Team 1 starts. Team 1 turns over their card and chooses their highest stat (statistic). Team 2 goes next. Team 2 turns their top card over and compares the chosen stat. Finally, Team 3 turns their top card over and compares the chosen stat. The team with the highest stat wins all three cards.

Example

Team 1 turns over their card and it is a USB flash drive. The USB flash drive has a portability rating of 5 stars, so Team 1 chooses this.

Team 2 turns over their top card and reveals a CD. The portability rating for the CD is 4 stars, which is lower than the USB flash drive.

Team 3 turns over their top card and reveals an internal hard disk. The portability rating for the internal hard disk is 1 star, which is lower than both the CD and USB flash drive.

The device with the highest portability rating is the USB flash drive, so Team 1 wins all three cards.

The winning team is the first team to win ALL the cards.

Note: In the case of a draw, the first player must choose the next highest stat on their card.

Taking it further

While it's not essential that the students play the game, it would feel like a crime not to, after all their hard work and effort! Have the students print out their cards prior to the next lesson and use the game as a starter to consolidate learning.

Little Man Computer

'Little Man Computer is a great way to explore low-level languages!'

Little Man Computer (LMC) is a simulator that models the basic features of a modern computer that uses Von Neumann architecture.

Teaching tip

It is highly recommended that you test out the simulator with the sample instruction set prior to the lesson to gain a better understanding of how the simulator works.

Taking it further

Challenge students to write a program to subtract two numbers.

The LMC can be programmed in machine code or assembly code. Begin by loading 'Little Man Computer' (peterhigginson.co.uk/LMC) and explain to students that the main function of the central processing unit (CPU) is to fetch and execute instructions. Load the following set of instructions (to add two numbers) into the simulator to demonstrate how it works:

Address	Instruction
00	INP
01	STA 99
02	INP
03	ADD 99
04	OUT
05	HLT

Share the above instructions with the students and ask them to load them into the simulator. Cut the following into strips and ask the students to match each description to the correct instruction.

Input a number and put it in the calculator
Store the number in the calculator in memory slot 99
Input a number and put it in the calculator
Add the number in slot 99 to the number in the calculator
Output the number that is now in the calculator
Halt

Discuss the answers with the students before challenging them to add three numbers using LMC.

Features of a CPU (a lesson using DART)

'Sir, this is meant to be a computer science lesson, not an English lesson!'

I often find that we can learn a lot from other subjects when teaching computer science, particularly other STEM subjects, such as science and maths. One method often used in English to support literacy, which lends itself well to computing, is DART.

Prior to the lesson, prepare a brief presentation introducing students to the main purpose and key features of the CPU. As a minimum, I would include number of cores, cache memory, clock speed and fetch-execute cycle. Ensure that the text inside the presentation is suitable for the reading ability of your class!

Print a set of key words and cut them out. You could tape them to the underneath of chairs for random distribution or, as I usually do, fold them into little pieces and place them in a jar or bag for the students to pick out.

Run the presentation so that students skim and scan the text (just as they would do with a textbook). If using PowerPoint, you can apply the 'appear' animation to the text (set to animate the text one letter at a time with a delay of 0.4 seconds between each letter) to give the appearance of a 'typewriter' effect.

At the end of the presentation, select students to pick a key word at random (or ask them to see whether there's one hidden under their chair) and either act out or draw the word that they have picked for the rest of the class to guess. I tend to split the students into teams and turn it into a competition.

Finish the activity by issuing a gap-fill exercise linked to the original text.

Teaching tip

The key here is to make the presentation brief and concise so as to allow the students to digest all the information.

Taking it further

For a bit of fun, you could also use a timer and give the opposing teams a chance to steal the points if the player's team doesn't guess it right within a minute.

Bonus idea ★

Other ways of using DART in the classroom are explored in Idea 13: DART your students.

Internet of things

'A great way to contextualise the importance of computer science is to have students explore the smart devices in their home!'

The internet of things (IoT) connects 'smart' devices over the internet and enables them to collect and exchange data. The internet of things has the potential to transform the way we live our lives, including how we work, how we stay fit and healthy, and how we reduce our carbon footprint. Having students explore the internet of things is a great way to demonstrate the impact that computer science can have on our everyday lives!

Taking it further

Have students design a 'smart home' that utilises the internet of things. Split the class into small groups and have each group focus on a particular room in the house.

Prior to the lesson, prepare some cards, each with a common household object on them — for example, fridge, door, mirror, wardrobe, light, thermostat, etc.

Start by asking the students to explain what they think is meant by the term 'internet of things'. Draw out answers such as 'smart homes', 'app-enabled appliances', 'wearable technology', etc. Inform the students that it is estimated that there are now more than 50 billion devices connected to the internet, from heating and lighting to wardrobes and fridges. Tell students that we call this the 'internet of things' or IoT for short.

Arrange the class into small groups. Provide each group with two of the pre-prepared cards (each containing a common household object) chosen at random. Challenge the students to think of a scenario where each object could be connected to the internet of things in order to solve an everyday problem — for example, a connected wardrobe that checks the weather forecast and suggests appropriate clothes to wear or a smart refrigerator that notifies you when you need to reorder items.

Bonus idea ★

If students have access to a Raspberry Pi, Arduino, Micro:bit, etc. and some sensors, challenge them to create a working prototype for their smart home.

#IoT

The great input/output QR hunt

'Miss, is a touch screen an input or output device?'

QR (quick response) codes are easy to create and have many uses in the classroom. One area of the computing curriculum where I have used QR codes with great success is input/output devices.

Prior to the lesson, prepare some QR codes (see Idea 19: Using QR codes) and hide them strategically around the classroom. I suggest fixing them to input/output devices associated with the QR code.

Divide students into teams of three or four and provide each team with a web-enabled device with QR-reading capability. Set a timer for 20 minutes and challenge students to find all the QR codes hidden around the classroom. Instruct students to take notes on what they find.

Once 20 minutes have elapsed, gather the students together and invite them to share what they have found.

Teaching tip

When preparing the QR codes, try to use a variety of different media types, and not just YouTube videos.

Taking it further

Challenge students to create their own QR code hunt by generating their very own QR codes using material that they have found on the internet.

Moral Machine

'A game of ethical and moral dilemma.'

Ethics can be a very dry subject to teach, but one way to make the topic more interesting is to turn it into a game!

Taking it further

Discuss with the class whether their decisions would have been different if presented with other characters (such as those with different political or religious views) and use this to explore the concept of bias.

The 'Moral Machine' (moralmachine.net) is a game created by the team at Massachusetts Institute of Technology (MIT) that explores the ethical and moral dilemmas involved in creating AI for driverless vehicles.

The game, which is based on the famous 'trolley problem', challenges players to choose who to save when the brakes fail on a driverless vehicle. The Moral Machine poses basic choices such as 'Should a self-driving car full of senior citizens crash to avoid a group of school children?' and 'Is it OK to run over two criminals in order to save one nurse?'

Inform the students that they are going to play a game that will explore the ethical and moral dilemmas faced in designing AI for driverless vehicles. Split the class into groups of four and explain to the students that they must work as a team through each of the scenarios. Encourage the students to debate their position before taking a vote on each scenario. Facilitate discussion on the results and note any similarities or differences between each of the teams' decisions (using the statistics from Moral Machine).

Bonus idea ★

Have students create their own scenarios, such as cats vs dogs, etc.

Computational thinking

Part 5

Making the tea algorithm

'Sir, which comes first, milk or hot water?'

A great way I find to teach algorithm design (a key component of computational thinking) is to challenge students to write a set of step-by-step instructions for making a cup of tea!

Teaching tip

The purpose of this exercise is not for the students to guess the correct order but to reinforce the point that an algorithm is a sequence of instructions, as well as introducing the notion of subprograms or subroutines.

Taking it further

Challenge students to write an algorithm for an everyday routine that includes at least one subprogram/subroutine – for example, making a sandwich or getting to school.

Prior to the lesson, print and cut out some instructions for making a cup of tea (boil kettle, pour boiling water into cup, add sugar, add milk, stir, etc.). Challenge students to put the instructions into the correct order.

Pick students at random to explain their algorithms to the rest of the class and highlight the different solutions. Explain that any given problem can have many different solutions!

Choose one of the students' algorithms and highlight the step 'boil the kettle'. Ask students, 'What is wrong with this instruction?' Draw out answers such as, 'What if you didn't know how to boil the kettle?', 'What if there is no water in the kettle?', etc. Use these answers to identify the need for subprograms/subroutines. Inform the students that some instructions can be broken up further into subprograms or subroutines and that, in a programming context, these are sometimes also referred to as functions or procedures.

Explain to the students that program code can be easier to read and understand if it is broken up into smaller sections. Inform the students that by breaking a program up into these sections (or subprograms), code can be made shorter, simpler and easier to debug.

Place the students into pairs and challenge them to write a subprogram/subroutine for boiling the kettle or taking milk out of the fridge, etc. Once complete, share some of the students' examples with the whole class.

Teaching with magic

'Pick a card, any card!'

All magic tricks are based on an algorithm (a sequence of step-by-step instructions). Similar to a recipe or set of directions, if any of the steps are not clearly explained, the trick is likely to fail. As well as introducing students to algorithm design, magic tricks can also help students to understand other key principles such as abstraction, pattern recognition and decomposition.

Probably the easiest trick to master is the 'Kings, Queens, Jacks and Aces' card trick (also known as the 'Royal Family'). A quick internet search will reveal lots of guides/how-to videos on how to perform this simple trick.

Start by demonstrating the trick to the class. This can be done using a video or, preferably, performed by you! After demonstrating the trick, divide the students into small groups and give each group a set of playing cards. Challenge the students to repeat the trick and, once they think they have mastered it, produce a step-by-step guide on how to perform the trick. Try to encourage the students to write down every step — this is key for the next part.

As the students write their step-by-step instructions, circle around the class and test out some of their instructions. Note: The key here is to be pedantic when following instructions, i.e. emphasise any imprecise or vague instructions. For example, in the case of the 'Royal Family' trick, if a student writes down the instruction 'Sort the cards into four suits', do this for every card in the pack and not just the jack, queen, king and ace. This should hopefully encourage the students to improve their instructions and to try to 'beat the teacher' — the aim being to highlight the importance of detailed and precise instructions when writing computer programs.

> **Teaching tip**
>
> Encourage the students to practise each trick with all the cards face up; this will help them to understand how the trick works.

#MagicOfTeaching

Crazy characters

'You told me to draw a circle, but you never said how big!'

One way to reinforce the importance of clear and precise instructions when writing code is to challenge students to write a simple set of instructions for drawing a 'crazy character'!

Teaching tip

The key to the success of this activity is to be pedantic when following the students' instructions! This will encourage students to refine and improve their instructions.

Taking it further

Time permitting, challenge the students in their pairs to design their own 'crazy character' and write a set of instructions for drawing it.

Put students into pairs and ask each pair to sit with their backs to one another. Give one student in each pair an activity card (containing a simple character design and set of instructions) and the other a pen and paper or mini-whiteboard. Example instructions:

• Create a circle for the body.
• Add two eyes.
• Add four legs.
• Add a mouth.
• Add a tooth.

Inform the students with the activity cards that they must read out their instructions to their partner, who must try to recreate their character using instructions alone. After five minutes, ask the students to compare their drawings with the original and to note down any similarities/differences between the two images.

Ask: 'Why are all the drawings so different to the originals?' Draw out answers such as, 'Not enough detail in the instructions' and 'The instructions need to be more precise'. Ask the students to suggest ways to improve the instructions and make a note of these.

Set a timer for 15 minutes and challenge the students, in their designated pairs, to improve the instructions on the activity cards. Once the time is up, select pairs at random to read their instructions out aloud for you to follow, ensuring that you follow their instructions exactly while drawing their character on a whiteboard or flipchart for the class to see.

Puzzle me

'Miss, I'm puzzled!'

One way to provide students with the opportunity to practise computational thinking skills (decomposition, pattern-matching, abstraction and algorithm design) is to have them solve puzzles.

Cube challenge

A two-cube calendar is a desk calendar consisting of two cubes with faces marked with digits 0 to 9. Students are challenged to fill in the gaps on two cube nets so that it is possible to arrange the cubes to represent any chosen day of the month (from 01 through to 31). Both cubes must be used at all times — for example, to represent day seven, both 0 and 7 must be visible. Example solution:

Taking it further

Have students test their puzzle-solving skills by entering them in the Bebras UK challenge (www.bebras.uk), a competition aimed at raising awareness of computer science by challenging players to solve computational thinking puzzles.

	4		
0	1	2	3
	5		

	8		
6	2	1	0
	7		

Note: While at first it appears that there are not enough sides for all the numbers, students will eventually realise that the 6 doubles as a 9 when turned upside down.

Word ladders

Word ladders were invented by Lewis Carroll, author of *Alice in Wonderland*. Students are given a start word and end word and, by progressively altering a single letter at a time, they must change the start word into the end word. Each word in the ladder must be a valid English word and must have the same length. Often the start word and end word are related. For example, to turn 'COLD' into 'WARM', one possible ladder could be: COLD → CORD → WORD → WARD → WARM.

Bonus idea ★

Have students attempt to solve other popular puzzles such as Sudoku, 'camel crossing', 'river-crossing conundrum', Tower of Hanoi, etc.

Human robot

'Miss, can I stop spinning around now?'

When exploring algorithms through physical activities such as movement and dance, students will encounter the same problems as when writing code. Encountering these problems through play can help to alleviate some of the anxiety felt by students when coding for the first time, and can also help them to become more resilient when faced with problems in the future.

Teaching tip

To reinforce the idea that the students are writing algorithms, print and laminate some large Scratch-like blocks for students to write instructions on using whiteboard pens.

Display the terms 'Repeat' and 'Loop' and ask the students to suggest each of the words' meanings. Draw out answers such as 'something that is done more than once', 'something that starts again from the beginning when it has finished', etc.

Display these words and definitions:

- **Repeat:** an action that is done more than once.
- **Loop:** a sequence that starts again from the beginning once it finishes.

Introduce the idea of repetition by identifying everyday 'repeats' that the students may have already encountered – for example, dance, repetitive songs, etc. Encourage students to discuss this with their partners and come up with some more examples.

Introduce students to counted loops, where all repeated actions are indented. For example:

```
Loop 4 times
    Stand
    Sit
```

Ask the students to perform the loop as a class before challenging them to create their own counted loop examples in pairs. Students should act out their instructions, with each pair taking it in turns to take on the role of programmer and 'human robot'.

A-maze-ing algorithms

'Miss, why have you put masking tape all over the floor?'

A great way to explore the importance of clear and precise instructions is to have students write an algorithm to solve a simple maze.

Start the lesson by drawing a simple maze on the classroom floor using masking tape, or chalk if planning to deliver the lesson outside. Ask for two volunteers and inform them that one of them will be blindfolded! Tell the first volunteer that they are going to act as the 'robot', and their challenge is to navigate their way through the maze while blindfolded, by following a simple set of verbal instructions. Inform the second volunteer (programmer) that their task is to guide the human robot through the maze by only using the commands forward, back, left turn and right turn.

Once the volunteers have successfully navigated the maze, ask the students why the robot found it difficult to follow the instructions. Draw out answers such as 'the instructions were too vague' or 'the instructions were not specific'. Ask students how they could improve their algorithm.

Share with students a simple maze design on paper (you could use a free online maze-generator such as www.mazegenerator.net) and challenge them to write an algorithm to successfully navigate the maze. To add a competitive element (gamification), challenge students to solve the maze using the smallest number of instructions possible. Alternatively, you can have students create their own mazes on paper or using masking tape or chalk.

Bonus idea ★

Have students create an algorithm for an autonomous bot that can solve any maze.

20 questions

'Are you Donald Trump?'

A fun way to have students explore the efficiency of different searching algorithms is to have them play a game of '20 questions'.

Teaching tip

Explain that the secret to playing '20 questions' is to ask questions that rule out half the possibilities each time.

Start by asking ten volunteers to line up in alphabetical order of surname. Next, ask for volunteers to explain how a linear search might work (i.e. sequentially checking each item in a list until a match is found or the whole list has been searched). Raise the question of what the problem might be if we had a hundred or even a thousand items in our list. Ask the students whether they can think of a better way. Inform them of a method called 'divide and conquer' – an algorithm often used as a strategy for solving large problems, by breaking them into smaller sub-problems.

Think of a famous person and ask the class to try to guess who you are thinking of by only asking questions with yes/no answers. They are allowed to ask a maximum of 20 questions, so they must think carefully before choosing. Ask for a volunteer to keep a record of the questions asked and another to keep count. Once the students have either guessed correctly or used up all their questions, go through their answers and identify any good questions, such as, 'Are you male/female?', etc. Ask the students to explain why these make a good first question.

Bonus idea ★

Play 'Mystery Skype'! Mystery Skype is a global guessing game, usually played over the internet via Skype or Hangouts, which epitomises the divide and conquer approach to questioning. In Mystery Skype, two teams have to guess the other's location by asking only yes/no-answer questions.

Inform the students that if they were to choose a question such as, 'Are you Donald Trump?' as their first question, they only rule out one possibility (great if they're right!), but by adopting the divide and conquer method, e.g. 'Are you male/female?', they can improve their search algorithm massively by ruling out half the possibilities.

Breaking the code

'Develop your students' problem-solving skills with some code-breaking challenges.'

As well as being fun and engaging, code breaking (or decryption) fosters problem-solving and enables students to practise key computational thinking skills.

Start by sharing a simple Caesar shift cipher with a shift of 1 – for example: IFMMP XPSME. Explain how a Caesar shift cipher works by replacing each plaintext letter with a different one that is a fixed number of places (known as a shift) down the alphabet. For example, using a shift of 1, A would become B, B would become C, etc. Inform the students that a Caesar cipher is a form of encryption. Challenge the students to decipher the cipher text. Answer: HELLO WORLD

Next, share the following clue: 'There are only _ types of people in the world: those who understand binary and those who don't.' Accompany it with this Caesar shift cipher: 'IYE YXVI RKFO DGOXDI WSXEDOC DY CKFO DRO GYBVN'. Challenge the students to decipher the encrypted message. Answer: YOU ONLY HAVE TWENTY MINUTES TO SAVE THE WORLD

Set the scene – for example, a virus is threatening to end the world – and place a laptop in a prominent position with a timer displayed (set for 20 minutes). Inform the students that in order to stop the virus and prevent world annihilation, they must unlock the laptop by deciphering a series of encrypted messages. Start the timer and password-protect the laptop. Share with the students some encrypted clues using a variety of different ciphers (e.g. Caesar shift, pigpen, scytale, substitution cipher, etc.). Explain that when pieced together, each of the clues will reveal the password for the laptop.

Teaching tip

Some students will identify that the missing number is the key to solving the cipher, whereas others will decipher the message by process of elimination.

Teaching tip

The periodic table of elements makes for an excellent substitution cipher. For example, to make the word 'use', you would use the atomic numbers 92 (U: Uranium) and 34 (Se: Selenium).

Bonus idea ★

Challenge the students to create their own encrypted message using their favourite cipher.

Origami algorithms

'Make computing relevant by using "real-life" algorithms!'

You can use algorithms to help describe everyday things. A great example is to have students write an algorithm for folding a paper aeroplane or origami animal.

Taking it further

Think about what parts of the origami animal or object are missing from the real animal or object that it is meant to represent, and use this as an example to explore abstraction.

Place the students into pairs and provide each pair with some blank paper and scissors. Challenge them to make their best paper aeroplane design – one they think will fly the furthest. Once the students have finished building their models, challenge them to write step-by-step instructions for recreating their design. Encourage the pairs to test their instructions continually as they write.

Next, have the students swap their completed plane algorithms with the pair next to them and try to recreate each other's plane designs using the instructions provided. Inform the students that they are allowed to get help from the other team if they get stuck, but the other team is not allowed to touch their paper plane. As the pairs try to follow each other's instructions, circulate the room and check that the students are continually debugging the instructions and fixing mistakes where necessary. Time permitting, allow the students to test out their finished paper aeroplanes.

Finish the activity by discussing with the class what they learned. Facilitate discussion by asking questions such as:

Bonus idea ★

As the title suggests, this also works for simple origami too. Have the students create a set of step-by-step instructions for creating a simple origami animal.

- Were you able to make a working paper plane from the other team's algorithm?
- What improvements did you make to the other team's algorithm? Why?
- How would you improve the activity?
- What important lessons did you learn from the activity?

#OrigamiAlgorithms

Guess the object

'Getting students to model, draw or mime a variety of different objects can help them to understand the concept of abstraction.'

Abstraction involves filtering out (ignoring) the unimportant details and focusing only on the essential characteristics.

Start by placing the students into teams of three or four. Give each team a set of pre-prepared challenge cards (that show the words 'draw', 'model' or 'mime') and some crafting materials (modelling clay, paper, coloured pencils, drinking straws, sticky tape, etc.).

Ask each team to decide who is going to play first and give each team a selection of pre-prepared 'guess the object' cards. Inform the teams that each player must take it in turns to pick up an object card and a challenge card. They then try to get the rest of the team to guess what is on the object card, using the method on the challenge card. For example, if the challenge card says 'draw' and the object card says 'tiger', the player must attempt to draw a tiger and challenge the rest of the team to guess what it is. As the students play the game, instruct them to record (using a table) which key features were included in the drawing, model or mime and which features were ignored.

Once the students have had at least two goes each at drawing, modelling or miming an object, stop the class and compare examples of what was included and what was excluded for the same object from two different teams. Explain to the class that this is a form of abstraction and that when abstracting, certain details are discarded but others are kept. Inform the students that abstraction is an important element of computational thinking, as it helps us to form a general overview of what the problem is and how we can solve it.

Teaching tip

As students are playing, circulate the room and encourage the students to think carefully about what was included, what was ignored and why.

Taking it further

Give the students some simple puzzles (see Idea 45: Puzzle me) and have them identify the key points or describe the problem in the smallest amount of words.

Bonus idea ★

To add a different spin on the activity, set a time limit, limit the number of allowed guesses or allocate points for guessing correctly.

Unplugged activities

Part 6

Image compression

'Miss, all those numbers are making my eyes go funny!'

Compression is the method that computers use to make files smaller by reducing the number of bits (1s and 0s) used to store the information. One form of compression is called 'lossless compression'. A great way to demonstrate how lossless compression works is with a fun unplugged activity!

Taking it further

Provide students with some blank 12 x 8 grids and challenge them to create their own pixel art image using lossless compression.

Start by displaying the following sequence:
3,1,5,1,3
4,1,3,1,4
3,7,3
2,2,1,3,1,2,2
1,11,1
1,1,1,7,1,1,1
1,1,1,1,5,1,1,1,1
4,2,1,2,4

Explain that the first number in each sequence refers to the number of white pixels and the next number in the sequence refers to the number of black pixels. Inform the students that if the first number is a 0, then the first pixel is black. Demonstrate this with the following example:
1, 2, 1, 2 = (1 x white), (2 x black), (1 x white), (2 x black)
0, 1, 1, 1, 2 = (1 x black), (1 x white), (1 x black), (2 x white)

Challenge students to recreate the image using the sequence above. Once the students have successfully recreated the image, display the same image using binary (see Idea 58). Ask the students to explain which representation is better. Draw out answers such as 'the first method is easier to read and uses up less space'.

Bonus idea ★

Ask students to swap their compressed pixel art with a neighbour and challenge them to recreate each other's images.

Inform students that we can make large files such as images smaller using a process called 'compression' and that the above example uses a method called 'lossless compression'.

Bubble sort dance algorithm

'Sir, do we have to do the dance bit?'

One basic type of sorting algorithm is called a bubble sort. A fun way to demonstrate how a bubble sort works is via the medium of Hungarian folk dance!

How it works

Prepare ten sheets of paper, each numbered from 1 to 10, and share the following video: www.youtube.com/watch?v=lyZQPjUT5B4

Ask for ten volunteers and have them stand at the front of the classroom. Ask for one more volunteer to be the sorter. Mix up the numbered sheets of paper and give each student a number at random. Instruct the students to hold the paper facing outwards so that their number is visible to the rest of the class. Explain to the students that each of them represents a value in an array. Provide the sorter with a list of instructions to follow:

How to bubble sort

1 Compare the first two students.
2 If the student on the right is holding a smaller number than the student on the left, ask them to swap places.
3 Move to the next pair of students.
4 Repeat steps 2 and 3 until you reach the end of the line.
5 When you reach the end of the line, repeat steps 1 to 4 until all of the students are in the correct order.

At the end of the activity, facilitate discussion by asking questions such as, 'How could you improve the algorithm?' or 'What is a better way to sort the list?'

Teaching tip

The students don't have to do the dance routine in order to complete the challenge, but it's so much more fun if they do! You can also laminate the numbered sheets of paper so that you can use them again.

Bonus idea ★

Challenge students to come up with their own sorting algorithm and compare it against the bubble sort for speed and accuracy.

World Wide Web unplugged

'Sir, can I be the server?'

A great way to explore how the World Wide Web works is to have students role-play what happens when a user enters an address in a web browser. Note this works best in a large hall or playground.

Teaching tip

To demonstrate what HTML code looks like, load up a web page in a browser, such as www. youtube.com, and show students the HTML source code. Instructions for Chrome: Right click → view page source. Instructions for Safari: Click on Develop tab → show page source.

Teaching tip

The main aim of this activity is to explain the difference between the internet and the World Wide Web.

Preparation

Prepare the following cards. I recommend cutting out and laminating them for reuse.

Server (IP: 216.58.213.110) x 1; Server (IP: 31.13.90.174) x 1; Server (IP: 91.198.174.192) x 1; Router x 7; Client x 1; Blank IP x 3; www.instagram.com (IP: Blank) x 1; www.youtube.com (IP: Blank) x 1; www.wikipedia.org (IP: Blank) x 1; DNS server card x 1 (with the following 'lookup' table attached to the reverse of the card).

URL	Server IP address
www.youtube.com	216.58.213.110
www.instagram.com	31.13.90.174
www.wikipedia.org	91.198.174.192

Next, print some screenshots of the following web pages: YouTube, Wikipedia, Instagram. (Note: These should NOT be laminated, as they will be cut up into pieces to represent 'packets'.)

Set-up

Start by asking the students, 'What is the internet?' Draw out answers such as 'globally connected network of computers', etc. Follow this by asking the students to explain what the World Wide Web is. Explain that the World Wide Web is a huge collection of documents written in HTML (HyperText Markup Language) that can be accessed using the internet.

Evenly distribute the students using all available space and hand out the pre-prepared cards. Explain to the students that they are going to act out what happens when a user types a web address into a browser.

Teaching tip

If you have more students than cards, the extra students can take on the role of additional routers.

Instructions

Give each student a card. Instruct the student holding the 'Client' card to pick one of the web address (URL) cards and pass it to the student holding the 'DNS server' card. Explain that this represents a user entering a web address (or 'URL') into a web browser.

Ask the student holding the DNS server card to look up the IP address for the URL they have been given, using the table printed on the back of their card, and to write the IP address in the blank space provided. The student must then pass the card back to the client. Inform the students that when a user types a web address into a browser, a request is sent to a DNS 'domain name system' server, which looks up the address in a table and returns its unique 12-digit-number 'IP address'.

Instruct the student holding the client card to pass the URL request card to the nearest router. Ask the students with the router cards to pass the URL request card to the server with the matching IP address via the quickest route.

When the 'request card' reaches the correct server, ask the student holding the card to cut the relevant web page into four pieces and pass the pieces to the nearest router. Ask the students holding the router cards to pass the individual pieces via different routes back to the client. Explain that when the server receives a request, it breaks the page into smaller pieces called 'packets' and sends these broken-up packets of data via multiple routes across the internet until they all reach the client.

Finally, ask the client to piece together the strips of paper using tape. Explain that when the client receives all the packets, the client's web browser reassembles the packets and translates this into a web page.

Intelligent piece of paper (AI)

'Let's play a game of noughts and crosses!'

A game of noughts and crosses is a fun way to introduce artificial intelligence (AI) and to reinforce the concept of algorithms.

Teaching tip

Have Player 1 read out each instruction loudly, so that the whole class can hear, before executing each move.

Taking it further

Challenge students to create an algorithm for another game – for example, to get the highest score in 2048, win a game of Connect 4® or solve a Rubik's Cube.

Start by asking for two volunteers to play a game of noughts and crosses. Have Player 1 read out the following to the class:
'I am a highly intelligent piece of paper. Let's play noughts and crosses. I am X and I go first...'

Hand Player 1 the 'intelligent piece of paper', containing the instructions below, and have them follow the instructions exactly. Inform Player 2 that they can make any move they wish, as long as it's within the rules of the game.

Move 1:
Place an X in any corner square.
Move 2:
If the other player did not go there THEN place an X in the opposite corner to move 1. ELSE place an X in any free corner square.
Move 3:
If there are 2 Xs and a space in a line THEN place an X in that space.
ELSE if there are 2 Os and a space in a line THEN place an X in that space.
ELSE place an X in any free corner.
Move 4:
If there are 2 Xs and a space in a line THEN place an X in that space.
ELSE if there are 2 Os and a space in a line THEN place an X in that space.
ELSE place an X in any free corner.
Move 5:
Place an X in the free space.

After a couple of games, have students discuss whether the piece of paper actually demonstrates intelligence.

Envelope variables

'Demonstrate a simple program that uses variables and assignment by running them on a computer made entirely out of students.'

Understanding variables and assignment is critical to being able to code, but the concept is not as easy as you might think!

Start by sharing the following simple program:

```
shark1 = "baby"
shark2 = "mommy"
shark2 = shark1
```

Next, ask for a volunteer and hand them a blank envelope. Explain that the envelope represents a variable (a placeholder for pieces of information that can change). Inform the class that we need to give our variable a name, and have the student write the name 'shark1' clearly on the front of the envelope. Refer back to the code you shared at the start. Show that we used the = sign to name our first variable. Tell the students that next we must assign the variable with a value – in this case, 'baby'. Write the word 'baby' clearly on a piece of paper and place it inside the envelope.

Ask for a second volunteer. Repeat the previous step but, this time, name the variable 'shark2' and assign it the value 'mommy'. Explain that now we have 'initialised' our two variables, we can do something with the values stored in them. Refer back to the simple program. Explain that as well as storing values, we can also use variables to swap values.

Ask the volunteer holding the envelope labelled 'shark1' to tell you what's inside their envelope. On a blank piece of paper, copy what's written inside shark1's envelope. Ask 'shark2' to give you the contents of their envelope and immediately destroy it (tear it up, stamp on it, etc.) before giving the paper copy from shark1 to shark2.

Taking it further

Share some more examples of simple programs that use variables and ask the students to predict the outcome.

Bonus idea ★

Turn the activity into a game, with mini-whiteboards instead of envelopes, where the students representing the variables must keep score.

Card sort

'Higher or lower than a jack?'

An excellent way to teach sorting algorithms is to have students sort playing cards.

Taking it further

Repeat the activity several times, each time asking the students to swap their instructions with a neighbouring group.

Put the students into teams of four and give each team a complete suit of playing cards (without the ace). Next, give each team at random a challenge card containing a set of instructions for one of three sorting algorithms:

Bubble sort
1 Compare the first two cards.
2 If the card on the right is lower than the card on the left, swap both cards.
3 Compare the next two cards and repeat step 2.
4 Repeat steps 2 and 3 until you reach the end of the pack.
5 Repeat steps 1 to 4 until all the cards are in order.

Merge sort
1 Split the cards into two piles of six.
2 Split the two piles in half again (so you have four piles of three).
3 Sort each pile into numerical order and place each pile in a stack face up.
4 Compare the top cards in the first two piles.
5 Put the lowest-value card face down in a new pile.
6 Repeat steps 4 and 5 until both piles are in one stack.
7 Repeat steps 4 to 6 for the other two piles.
8 You should now have two piles. Repeat steps 4 and 5.

Insertion sort

1 Place a marker (e.g. pencil) between the first two cards.
2 If the card to the right of the marker is lower than the card on the left, swap both cards.
3 Move the marker one place to the right.
4 If the card to the right of the marker is lower than the card on the left, swap both cards.
5 If the cards to the left of the marker are not in order, keep swapping the cards on the left (moving from right to left) until they are all in order.
6 Repeat steps 3 to 5 until all the cards are in order.

Bonus idea

Turn the activity into a race, series of time trials or even a knockout tournament to see which sorting algorithm is the fastest/most efficient.

Binary representation of images (unplugged)

'A great way to explain how a computer represents images is to have children create pixel art using binary.'

One area of the computing curriculum that I find lends itself well to the unplugged approach is binary representation of images.

Teaching tip

To aid students, cross off each number in the binary sequence after they have placed their card on the table or floor.

Taking it further

Put the students into pairs and challenge them to create their own pixel art and convert it into binary (1s and 0s).

Bonus idea ★

Ask students to explore how a four-colour image could be represented using binary.

Prior to the lesson, prepare a simple monochrome (black and white) pixel art image, such as a character, symbol or game sprite. A quick internet search will provide lots of inspiration. Once you've decided on a theme, convert your image into binary by replacing each white space with a '0' and each black space with a '1'.

In the lesson, ask the students to stand in a line and place on the floor (or table) a stack of white and black cards (preferably cut into squares). Share the binary representation of the image you prepared earlier and explain that each 0 represents a white card and each 1 represents a black card. Instruct the students, in turns, to pick up the corresponding coloured card for the next number in the sequence (starting from left to right and top to bottom) and place it in the corresponding position on the floor. Once the last card has been placed, share the original image before it was converted into binary and compare it to the students' solution.

Explain that an image is made up of tiny dots called pixels and that each pixel (short for picture element) represents one colour. You could share an image that has been zoomed in to reveal the individual pixels. Inform the students that a computer stores each pixel as a series of 0s and 1s (called binary). Explain that, in this example, the computer stored each white pixel as a 0 and each black pixel as a 1.

How computers work

'This simulation gives students a basic sense of how computers work.'

In this activity, students take on the role of various parts of a computer and simulate the running of a simple program.

Prepare the following three worksheets:
1 **CPU:** (a) Add 1 to x; (b) Plot x and y; (c) Add 2 to x; (d) Plot x and y; (e) Subtract 3 from x; (f) Add 1 to y; (g) Plot x and y; (h) Add 2 to x; (i) Plot x and y; (j) Add 2 to x; (k) Plot x and y; (l) Subtract 4 from x; (m) Add 1 to y; (n) Plot x and y; (o) Add 4 to x; (p) Plot x and y; (q) Subtract 3 from x; (r) Add 1 to y; (s) Plot x and y; (t) Add 2 to x; (u) Plot x and y; (v) Subtract 1 from x; (w) Add 1 to y; (x) Plot x and y.
2 **ALU/memory:** 2 x 26 table containing the headings x and y and the first values set to 0.
3 **Display:** 5 x 5 grid with the numbers 0 to 4 along the x (left to right) and y (top to bottom) axes.

Attach these instructions to each worksheet:
1 **CPU:** Instruct the other components (ALU, display) what to do by executing mathematical instructions such as 'Add 2 to x', 'Subtract 1 from y' and 'Plot x and y', etc.
2 **ALU/memory:** Perform simple addition and subtraction operations on x and y coordinates, as instructed by the CPU, and pass these on to the display.
3 **Display:** Plot (shade in) the corresponding x and y coordinates stored in the ALU/memory.

Split the class into groups of three and hand out the pre-prepared worksheets. Assign each student, in each group, one of the three roles (CPU, ALU, display) and ask them to follow the instructions on their designated worksheet.

Teaching tip

Get the students to sit with their backs facing each other until the CPU has finished running the program and the display is ready to reveal their image.

Bonus idea ★

Challenge students to design their own 5 x 5 pixel art image and write a set of instructions for the CPU to execute.

Memory

'Miss, can I be the CPU?'

A great way to explore how data is transferred between different storage locations inside a computer, such as RAM, cache memory, secondary storage and virtual memory, is with this fun unplugged activity!

Taking it further

Use this activity to explore other concepts such as memory addressing, the fetch execute cycle, assembly-level programming and Little Man Computer.

Preparation

Prior to the lesson, tape off the room (using masking tape, or chalk if delivering the activity outside) to create five separate zones. Prepare and label each of the zones as follows:

- Secondary storage: four rows of five chairs placed near the back of the room.
- Virtual memory: one row of five chairs placed directly in front of the four rows (secondary storage).
- CPU: single chair placed at the front of the room.
- Cache memory: two chairs placed next to the CPU.
- RAM: four chairs placed somewhere between the CPU and virtual memory.

Set-up

Give each student a number at random and ask them to sit in any of the four rows of chairs (secondary storage). Choose one student to take on the role of the CPU and three students to be the 'buses' – one who must walk slowly (pigeon steps), one who must walk at a medium pace and one who must move very quickly.

How it works

Step 1: Accessing data from the hard disk drive (HDD) without the use of RAM

Have the student who is acting as the CPU request that the student representing the slow bus find the student with number 1 (first instruction) from the secondary storage. When the student acting as the slow bus finds the student with number 1, they must return the number to the CPU.

Step 2: Loading data from HDD into RAM

Reset the secondary storage area (i.e. give the numbered instructions back to their original owners). Move the students with the first four instructions into the RAM seats. Have the CPU repeat the process of requesting instructions, only this time the medium-speed bus is used to retrieve the numbers from the students in the RAM chairs. The difference in access time should be emphasised. The slow bus can be used at this point to transfer the next available instruction into the empty RAM seats, albeit at a slower rate.

Step 3: Introducing cache memory

Reset the numbers as follows:

• numbers 1 and 2 in the cache memory seats
• numbers 3 to 6 in the RAM seats.

Have the CPU repeat the process of requesting instructions; however, on this occasion, it should start by requesting numbers from the cache memory seats using the fast bus. While this is being done, the medium bus transfers the next instruction from RAM to cache memory (at a slower pace than the fast bus) and the slow bus continues to refill the RAM seats from secondary storage.

Step 4: Utilising virtual memory to increase speed

Reset the students one final time. Repeat step 3, only this time using two buses working together. Instruct the slow bus to transfer data from the virtual memory seats to the RAM seats and the medium-speed bus from RAM to the processor. Explain that when we don't have enough RAM, we can use virtual memory to increase speed.

Bonus idea

Demonstrate how increasing the amount of RAM might help to improve performance by moving extra chairs into the RAM area and repeating step 3.

Network topologies

'Use string and various other props to enable students to simulate the various network topologies required for GCSE computing.'

A network's topology is the arrangement in which all the nodes (devices) on a network are connected together. A great way to explore the different topologies is to have students act out passing messages across different network configurations.

Teaching tip

For each network configuration, ask the students to discuss the following:

- Which is most reliable and why?
- What happens when a cable breaks?
- What happens when a computer breaks?
- What are the security risks?

Start by asking two volunteers to hold a piece of string (one at each end). Give the students a toilet roll tube or similar object with 0001 written on it, and challenge them to work out how to send the number over the piece of string. Ask the students to explain how they would send a larger number, e.g. 255, and how they would know when the whole message had been successfully received.

Split the class into groups of four or five and, using pieces of string and toilet roll tubes, challenge them to come up with different ways to send the message to several computers.

Next, using the string and toilet roll tubes, have students act out the three most common topologies:

- **Bus network:** Two students act as terminators, holding the piece of string at each end, while others stand in line acting as the nodes, with one hand on the piece of string.
- **Ring network:** Students stand in a circle with a string between them while passing the message to each other in one direction only.
- **Star network:** One student acts as a central computer with all others connected directly to it. The central computer acts as a postal service, passing all the messages on.

Taking it further

Using what they have learned about different networking topologies, have students dive deeper and explore other areas of networking, such as protocols, data collision and reliability.

Data representation

Part 7

Binary addition

'01 + 01 = 11'

Binary addition works in very much the same way as normal addition, except that it carries over a value of 2 instead of a value of 10.

Taking it further

Have students attempt some simple pre-prepared 4-bit binary sums (showing their working out).

Start with a simple sum (adding two denary numbers) for the students to solve, e.g.:

	1	2			1	2
+	1	8	+		1	8
					3	0
			carry	1		

Next, introduce a simple binary sum, e.g.:

	0	1			0	1
+	1	0	+		1	0
					1	1

Explain that we add binary numbers in the same way as denary numbers. However, we carry groups of 2 instead of 10, e.g.:

	0	1			0	1
+	0	1	+		0	1
					1	0
			carry	1		

Share the following binary sum on the board. Challenge the students to solve it and identify the problem:

	1	0	1	1			1	0	1	1
+	1	1	0	0	+		1	1	0	0
							0	1	1	1
					carry	1				

Explain that if we only have 4 bits to store the result, there would be no room for the final carry – resulting in the wrong answer. Explain that when there isn't room to store the resulting calculation, we get an error, which we call overflow.

Binary numbers

'There are 10 types of people in the world: those who understand binary and those who don't!'

The circuits in a computer's processor are made up of billions of transistors (tiny switches that can be activated by an electronic signal). The digits 1 and 0 used in binary represent the 'on' and 'off' state of a transistor. A great way to demonstrate this principle is with a fun unplugged activity courtesy of csunplugged.org!

Prior to the lesson, prepare five cards with the following sequence of dots: Card 1: one dot; Card 2: two dots; Card 3: four dots; Card 4: eight dots; Card 5: 16 dots.

Start by asking for five volunteers and have them line up. Hand out Card 1 (one dot) to the volunteer furthest to the right. Explain that they are one 'bit' (binary digit) and can be either 'off' (blank side of the card facing forward) or 'on' (dot-side facing forward).

Hand out Card 2 (two dots) to the next volunteer in line (person to the left) and ask them to reveal what's on the front of their card.

Hand out Card 3 (four dots) to the next volunteer in line but ask them to conceal what is on the front of the card. Ask the rest of the class to guess what number is on the concealed card (most students will probably guess 'three'). Ask the volunteer to reveal what is on their card and ask the class whether they can see a pattern. At this stage, some students may correctly identify that each number is doubling. Repeat this step for all the remaining cards (or until the students correctly identify the pattern).

Ask students what is wrong with this number system. Draw out answers such as 'there is no three' or 'no five', etc.

Teaching tip

When making the cards, mount them onto black paper or card. This will act as a visual aid to help students to understand that the card (or bit) is in the 'off' position when the black side is facing forward.

Taking it further

Ask students to discuss how we could make three and five using the cards. Have the volunteers holding Cards 1 and 2 show their cards. Explain that we can make three by simply adding Cards 1 and 2. Ask the students how they would make six or 31, etc.

Bonus idea ★

Challenge students, using the cards, to count from zero to 31 as fast as they can by flipping the cards in sequence.

Binary representation of images

'Sir, are we allowed to make a Pokémon?'

Art is a perfect medium for exploring complex concepts in computing. In this activity we use pixel art to explore binary representation of images.

Teaching tip

Have some example pixel art images to hand to share with students, so that time isn't wasted searching for ideas/inspiration!

Taking it further

Challenge students to create conditional formatting rules for a 2-bit (four-colour) or 4-bit (16-colour) image.

In this activity, students explore how to create pixel art using spreadsheet software such as Microsoft Excel, as well as learning advanced formatting techniques such as conditional formatting.

The following example assumes that you're using Microsoft Excel, but the principles should be the same for any other spreadsheet software.

- Start by opening a new workbook.
- Highlight all of the cells by clicking the 'Select all' button or by holding down Ctrl and A together.
- While all the cells are selected, set the height of each cell to 80 pixels and the width of each cell to 80 pixels.
- With all cells still selected, click on 'Conditional formatting' and select 'Highlight cell rules'.
- Select 'equal to' from the drop-down menu.
- Next, in the 'Format cells that are equal to' box, enter '0' and format with 'Custom format' and 'White'.
- Repeat the previous step for cells that are equal to '1' and format with 'Custom format' and 'Black'.
- Once the workbook has been set up, students can create images by entering the corresponding binary number, i.e. '0' for white and '1' for black, in each cell.

Binary representation of sound

'Please Sir, not Baby Shark again!'

Sound waves are analogue, so in order to store these waves digitally, we use an analogue-to-digital convertor (ADC).

To demonstrate how an ADC works, give students the following sample rates (taken at one-second intervals) and have them input the values into a spreadsheet and create a line graph (with markers). Sample data: 3.2, 3.9, 5, 6.5, 8, 9, 9, 8, 6, 4, 2.2, 1.8, 2.2, 4.5, 7, 7.4, 7, 4.5, 3, 3, 4.5

Next have the students create a column chart using the same data (if using Excel, I suggest using 'Quick style 8') and compare it to the original wave.

Have the students repeat the above activity for the following data sampled at half-second intervals. Ask them to compare the two sets of graphs and identify which column graph most closely matches the curve.

Sample data: 3.2, 3.5, 3.9, 4.4, 5, 5.8, 6.5, 7.2, 8, 8.6, 9, 9.1, 9, 8.7, 8, 7.1, 6, 5, 4, 3.2, 2.6, 2.1, 1.8, 1.8, 2.2, 3, 4.5, 6, 7, 7.3, 7.4, 7.3, 7, 6, 4.5, 3.5, 3, 2.9, 3

Inform students that the quality and size of the file is affected by two factors: sample rate and bit rate. Explain that the sample rate refers to the number of samples taken every second, and that the greater the frequency of the samples, the better the sound quality. For a visual example of this, see teachwithict.com/binary-representation-of-sound.html.

Teaching tip

To demonstrate the effects of sample rates, play two samples of the same track (I often choose something from popular culture), each compressed at different sample rates (one at 44100 and the other at 8000), using Audacity or similar.

Taking it further

Explain that the bit rate refers to the number of bits used to store each sample, and that the more bits that are sampled, the better the accuracy of the file but also the greater the file size.

Bonus idea ★

Share with students an MP3 file and have them open it in Audacity (or similar software) and zoom in to see the value of each sample.

Binary bingo

'On its own, number 1000!'

Whether used as a starter, plenary or revision exercise, binary bingo is a fun way to test students' understanding of binary representation of numbers.

Teaching tip

Laminate the bingo cards so that they can be reused in subsequent lessons or with other groups.

How it works

Prior to the lesson, prepare some bingo-style cards (I tend to use a 5 x 3 grid format) with eight numbers between 0 and 15 (converted to binary) placed at random on each card (see example below).

0000			1001	1100
	0100	0111		
0010	0101			1011

Note: No two cards should look the same.

Bonus idea ★

Flip the activity so that the denary numbers are written on the card and the teacher calls out random binary numbers.

At the start of the lesson, pair up students and give each pair one of the pre-prepared bingo cards. Call out a denary number between 0 and 15 and instruct the students to convert each number in their heads and cross out the binary equivalent if it appears on their card. The first pair to get a 'full house' is the winner!

It's all about hex

'Roses are #FF0000, violets are #0000FF, hex uses base 16, and is simpler than base 2.'

Hexadecimal (or hex) is a base 16 numbering system often used by programmers to simplify the binary system. With hex, an 8-bit binary number can be written using only two digits, making it easier to write and understand in comparison to binary.

Start by writing two numbers on the board, one in binary and one in hex – for example, 1101 1001 and C9. Ask students which is easiest to remember. Explain that the smallest value that we can have in 4 bits (nibble) is 0000 (0 in denary) and the largest value is 1111 (15 in denary), and that we need to represent each value with a single digit. Display the following table on the whiteboard and ask students to fill in boxes 2 to 9:

Denary: |0|1|2|3|4|5|6|7|8|9|10|11|12|13|14|15|
Hex: |0|1| | | | | | | | | | | | | | |

Inform students that we hit a problem when we reach 10. Ask the students to suggest ways in which we could represent the last six numbers without using numbers. Tell students that to get round this problem, we substitute the numbers 10 to 15 with the letters A to F, and that we call this number system hexadecimal (or hex for short). For example:

Denary: |0|1|2|3|4|5|6|7|8|9|10|11|12|13|14|15|
Hex: |0|1|2|3|4|5|6|7|8|9|A1|B1|C1|D1|E1|F1|

Demonstrate how to convert an 8-bit binary number to hex using the following example.

Denary   74 = 0 1 0 0 1 0 1 0 (binary)
Conversion: binary value split into groups of four digits 0 1 0 0 | 1 0 1 0 = 4 | 10 (A in hex)
Hex = 4A

Once the students understand the concept, have them convert some 8-bit binary values into hex.

Taking it further

Share with students a selection of colour codes used in web design – for example, #FFFFFF (white) and #000000 (black). Ask students to work out how many bits are required to store all 16,777,215 colours by converting #FFFFFF to binary. (Answer: 24)

IDEA 68

ASCII 'secret' agent

'0100 1001 0010 0000 0110 1100 0110 1111 0111 0110 0110 0101
0010 0000 0110 0010 0110 1001 0110 1110 0110 0001 0111 0010
0111 1001 0010 1110'

All characters, whether they are letters, symbols or numbers, are stored as binary numbers in a computer. All of the characters that a computer can use are called a character set. Two character sets most commonly used are ASCII and Unicode.

Taking it further

Challenge students to create their own secret messages to share with their classmates.

Prior to the lesson, prepare some secret messages converted to binary using an ASCII table. For example:

0100 1001 | 0010 0000 | 0110 1100 | 0110 1111 |
0111 0110 | 0110 0101 | 0010 0000 | 0110 0010 |
0110 1001 | 0110 1110 | 0110 0001 | 0111 0010 |
0111 1001 | 0010 1110

Answer: 'I love binary'

Start by explaining that characters are converted into binary using something called a character set. Inform students that one of the most commonly used character sets is ASCII (American Standard Code for Information Interchange) and show them an example.

ASCII	Dec	Binary
A	65	0100 0001
B	66	0100 0010
C	67	0100 0011
D	68	0100 0100

Explain that the ASCII character set uses 7 bits, which allows the computer to encode up to 128 characters.

Share with students the complete ASCII table (converted into binary) and challenge them to decipher the secret messages that you prepared prior to the lesson.

84

Exam
preparation

Part 8

Padlet

'It's like sticky notes, but online!'

Padlet (padlet.com) is an online noticeboard where students and teachers can collaborate, reflect and share ideas; it is an ideal platform for collating ideas and resources, perfect for when preparing for exams.

Teaching tip

By adding to the Padlet over time and for the duration of the course, you can very easily (and quickly) create a comprehensive revision resource for your students.

Taking it further

Padlet can be used in many ways, not just for revision. Use Padlet to create a timeline of influential people/ significant events in computing history or have the students create an interactive display showing the inside of a computer.

#Padlet

Padlet is essentially an online 'bulletin' board that enables students and teachers to collaborate, reflect, share ideas and collate resources via virtual 'sticky notes'. With Padlet, teachers can create group walls to share with their class or invite students to create their own walls. Padlet supports a wide variety of content, including images, documents, files from your computer and links to pages on the web. With Padlet, you can also embed content from anywhere on the web, including audio and video from popular platforms such as YouTube and Vimeo. Best of all, it's free!

While having a wide range of uses, Padlet is a perfect platform for collating resources in preparation for exams. Here are just a few potential uses:

- Create a discussion board for students to post questions about their computing exam.
- Post a question taken from a past paper and have the students build a model answer collaboratively.
- Create a repository of useful revision resources, including exam tips, videos and online quizzes; alternatively, have students create their own revision Padlet!
- Use Padlet to share model answers to past exam questions or provide strategies for responding to specific command words.

Round-robin revision

'Make revision fun and engaging with a series of mini games.'

These activities make for a perfect 'last-minute' cramming session.

Divide the room into three zones ('You bet', 'Heads up' and 'Memorise IT') and split the class into three. Explain to the students that they are going to take part in a series of 20-minute mini games that will test their subject knowledge.

1. You bet

Split the first table into two teams and place some challenge cards on the table face down, each containing a computing-related topic or key word. Instruct the students to turn over the top card. Each team has 20 seconds to bet how many terms they can list that are related to the given key word or topic. The team with the highest bet then has two minutes to list as many related terms as they can. If the team fails to reach the number they bet, the point goes to the opposing team.

2. Heads up

Place some challenge cards on the second table face down, each containing a computing-related topic or key word. Inform the students that without looking, they must take it in turns to pick up a card from the pile and place it on their forehead. The other students must then try to describe what is on the card. Each player has 60 seconds to guess what is on their card.

3. Memorise IT

Split the third group into two teams and place some pre-prepared A4-sized cards on the table face down, each containing up to 15 key words related to a different topic. Inform the students they each have 60 seconds to memorise all the key words on each card. The winning team is the team that can memorise the most key words.

> **Bonus idea** ★
>
> Have each team pick their best two players to play a game of 'Word tennis', in which the players from each team must take it in turns to say a word related to a given key word until one of them runs out of ideas.

Revision podcasts

'Create revision resources that students can listen to anytime, anywhere!'

Podcasts provide a wonderful opportunity for students to share their work with a global audience and, due to their portable nature, are a perfect medium for creating revision materials that students can access pretty much anytime, anywhere!

Teaching tip

Try to keep your podcasts to three to five minutes in length. If you need to go over that length of time, use chapters to break the podcast up.

A podcast is much like a radio show but, instead of being broadcast live, is pre-recorded and distributed over the internet, ready to be downloaded to a web-enabled device such as a smartphone, tablet or PC. Podcasts are easy to create, thanks to free tools such as Garageband (Mac/iOS) and Audacity (PC), and can be either hosted on the school's VLE or uploaded to a free online hosting service such as iTunes or Anchor.fm.

When creating your own podcasts, I recommend following these simple rules:

1 Start with some intro music (or a jingle).
2 Introduce the topic/theme.
3 Record the main content.
4 Summarise the key points.
5 Finish with some outro music.

Below are just a few examples of how to include podcasts in your revision toolkit:

- Create a revision resource to summarise a topic – for example, features of a CPU.
- Share exam advice on how to answer specific questions – for example, how to identify the command words.
- Share revision strategies, such as how to deal with stress or how to plan for revision.

Bonus idea ★

Have students create their own revision resource to summarise a topic.

PEE (point, evidence, explain)

'Sir, did you just tell us to PEE on our work?'

Acronyms are often used as mnemonic devices to remember key concepts or phrases. One such acronym, used to help improve the quality of written answers to questions, is PEE (point, evidence, explain).

'Point, evidence, explain', often abbreviated to PEE, is a writing formula used for answering questions. It provides a framework for students to build an argument and is often used whenever a student is expected to express an opinion or answer an essay-style question.

Teaching tip

PEE works best when introduced early, preferably in Year 7 or 8, and used regularly so that it becomes a natural process for the students.

Example

- **Point:** Start by making a point, conveying what you believe. For example, 'The internet is a good thing!'
- **Evidence:** Next, provide some evidence to support your point. For example, 'After the Boxing Day tsunami in 2004, bloggers and news outlets helped to raise money to support the victims of the disaster by sharing videos and news stories of the devastating effects of the tsunami online.'
- **Explain:** Finally, explain how the evidence you have provided proves the point that you are trying to make. For example, 'Because of the huge global online audience, more money was raised online than all of the governments' aid combined.'

PechaKucha

'20 slides, 20 seconds each — how difficult could it be?'

A PechaKucha is a great way to encourage students to be more concise and a little more creative with their presentations! It is also a perfect medium for consolidating learning and creating revision resources.

Teaching tip

Set a word limit — 50 to 60 words should be enough — so as to allow students to focus on the key points without missing any of the important detail.

I came across this little gem at a TeachMeet. The idea was originally conceived by Astrid Klein and Mark Dytham in 2003, as a way of presenting information related to architecture. Each presentation must contain no more than 20 slides and each slide must last for 20 seconds. Traditionally, a PechaKucha consists mainly of images, photos or graphics, with little to no text.

What I like about the PechaKucha approach is that it introduces students to 'abstraction' — abstraction is one of the four key components of computational thinking and involves filtering out (essentially ignoring) any unnecessary detail and focusing only on the key points. You can employ the PechaKucha approach as part of an ICT lesson to help students develop a more concise/professional approach to creating presentations; however, because the emphasis of a PechaKucha is to focus only on the key points, I find that they are the perfect medium for creating student-made revision resources!

Bonus idea ★

Rather than using traditional presentation software such as PowerPoint or Keynote, have students try something different, such as creating a Prezi or Powtoon.

#PechaKucha

Sketch-noting

'Sketch-noting is a great way to empower students and allows them to synthesise information visually.'

Visual cues aid memory by enhancing the recall process so it's no wonder that sketch-noting, a technique commonly used at conferences and keynotes, is finding its way into the classroom.

Sketch-noting is used to describe a form of visual note-taking or, more succinctly, purposeful doodling! Through a combination of pictures and embellishments, sketch-noting is primarily used to record key points while listening to a keynote or reading through text. It can also be used to express ideas or thoughts. Many students find sketch-noting and doodling help them to take in, organise and retain computing theory knowledge. Sketch-noting can also be used as a powerful revision and essay-planning tool! Thankfully, you don't need to be an artist to sketch-note and, with these simple tips, your students will soon be on their way to becoming sketch-noting masters!

Teaching tip

It is important to remind students that they don't need to be artists to sketch-note. I also recommend that you model best practice by sharing some examples of your own sketch-notes with your students.

- Master sketching common objects – let students practise common objects such as containers, place-holders and connectors!
- Practise! Practise! Practise! Have your students practise at home, perhaps while watching a YouTube video or reading a book.
- Latch onto quotes – quotes are often used in extended exam questions to reinforce an argument. Quotes are best written down in their entirety so as not to lose the original meaning, but can be embellished with banners, clouds or speech marks.
- Pace yourself – remind students that they don't have to draw everything they see or hear!
- Don't aim for perfection – the main purpose of a sketch-note is to aid recall, and therefore it doesn't have to be a work of art.

Bonus idea ★

Sketch-noting is not just a great revision tool; it can also be used to consolidate learning. Challenge your students to create a class sketch-note to sum up the key learning from a lesson as part of a plenary.

#SketchNotes

Command word bingo

'A simple starter activity that will pay dividends at exam time!'

One of the biggest barriers for students when answering extended questions is knowing what is expected of them. One simple strategy to help students identify the command words and understand their meaning is 'command word bingo'.

Teaching tip

Remember to tick off each command word as you read each definition so that you know which words you have used and are able to check these against the students' answers.

Prepare some bingo-style cards, each containing six command words chosen at random (see example below).

Justify		Compare
	Demonstrate	Identify
Analyse	Interpret	

At the start of the lesson, pair up students and give each pair one of the pre-prepared bingo cards. Call out a definition at random and challenge the students to match the definition to the corresponding command word on their cards. The first pair to get a 'full house' is the winner!

Definitions (taken from Ofqual's official computing list):

- calculate: work out the value of something
- compare: identify similarities and/or differences
- convert: change data from one form to another
- define: specify the meaning of
- describe: set out characteristics
- develop: take forward or build upon given information
- discuss: present key points
- draw: produce a diagram
- explain: set out purposes or reasons
- give: produce an answer from recall
- justify: support a case with evidence
- state: express in clear terms
- suggest: present a possible case/solution.

BUG hunt

'Help students to understand thoroughly what is expected of them during exams by getting them to deBUG each question.'

Not to be confused with debugging, BUG, like PEE (point, evidence, explain), is an acronym used to help students make the most of extended exam questions. BUG stands for box, underline, glance (or go back).

How it works

Box

First, ask students to draw a box around each of the command words. This will help them to identify what type of answer the examiner will be looking for!

Underline

Next, get the students to underline each of the key words; this allows them to identify which words to include in their answer.

Glance

Finally, get the students to glance/go back over the questions again to check that they have done what is expected from the 'boxed' words and included all the underlined words in their answer.

Teaching tip

Like all other revision strategies, the key to success is to start using this as early as possible and use it frequently, so that it becomes second nature!

Tweet IT

'Tweet your students with this fun revision strategy that will help them to remember key information.'

A great way to consolidate learning or revise for a topic is to get students to summarise what they have learned using only 280 characters or fewer.

Teaching tip

Laminate the Twitter cards so that you can use them more than once.

Anyone who has ever experienced using a micro-blogging platform such as Twitter will understand how much of a challenge it can be to convey your message when limited to just 280 characters. However, while being a challenge, I find that by limiting students to only 280 characters, it encourages them to be more concise and focus only on the key information – perfect for exam preparation. It also introduces students to the concept of abstraction – a key component of computational thinking.

How it works

- Prepare some Twitter-style cards for students to use to summarise the key points.
- Give the students some information on a chosen topic – for example, features of a CPU. This could be in the form of a DART activity (see Idea 13: DART your students), video, presentation, etc.
- Challenge the students to simplify and summarise the information using 280 characters or fewer (similar to a tweet).

Bonus idea ★

Use your school's Twitter account to tweet out your students' revision tweets leading up to their exam.

Revision speed dating

'A fun and engaging activity that gets students talking.'

I came across this wonderful idea at a TeachMeet in Scotland. The idea, originally meant as a literacy strategy to encourage students to ask and answer questions, is a perfect GCSE revision activity.

The idea is simple. Start by putting the students into pairs. Arrange all the pairs sitting facing each other in a circle. Give each pair a different topic card containing six questions (ideally questions from past exam papers) and a dice.

Set a timer for three minutes and inform the students that when the timer starts, they must choose a question at random by rolling their dice. The pairs must then write down as much as they can on the topic or question. After each turn, get the students inside the circle to swap places with the person next to them and start all over again.

Teaching tip

While it's perfectly fine for the students to answer the same question more than once, you can mix things up a little by randomly getting the students to swap question cards with the person next to them or by providing 12 questions and a pair of dice.

Bonus idea

At the end of each turn, get the students to mark each other's answers.

Match IT

'A fun way to get students to revise for their exams.'

Make revision engaging and memorable by turning it into a game!

Prepare some cards, each containing a computing term and a definition. For example:

Social engineering 'Match IT'

- Blagging: The act of creating and using invented stories to gain a person's interest and encourage them to give away information about themselves.
- Phishing: A form of cyber-attack where criminals try to obtain sensitive information by sending emails (or SMS) purporting to be from reputable companies.
- Pharming: A form of online fraud where users are redirected to a bogus website in order to obtain personal information.

In addition to the definition cards, prepare some scenario cards, each containing a different scenario related to the chosen topic. For example: 'You receive an email from your bank asking you to check your most recent transactions. You click on the link in the email and it takes you to a fake website that is made to look like your bank's website.'

Start by giving each of the players a set of definition cards. Give the students time to read the definitions on each card. Next, shuffle the scenario cards and place them face down in a pile. The players must then take it in turns to turn over each scenario card and read aloud what is written on the card. As each scenario is revealed, the other players must try to match the correct definition card to the scenario. The first player to place down the correct definition card wins the scenario card. The player with the most scenario cards at the end of the game wins!

Bonus idea ★

As an alternative to the scenario cards, have the students match the definition cards to past exam questions instead.

Programming activities

Part 9

Magic 8-ball®

'Will I ever play for Manchester United?'

The Magic 8-ball® is a fortune-telling toy created by Mattel® in the 1950s. The game works by asking the 8-ball a yes or no question, to which the 8-ball will reply with 'Yes', 'No', 'Maybe', etc. While being fun and engaging, games such as the Magic 8-ball® are also great for introducing programming fundamentals such as iteration, selection and data structures.

Teaching tip

The example (right) is in Python but can easily be adapted for other programming languages.

Teaching tip

Start by explaining what each line of the code does and then challenge the students to write a program for simulating flipping a coin/rolling a dice, before attempting the 8-ball challenge.

Taking it further

Having long lists is not very efficient, and they also make it more difficult to debug. Challenge students to improve their game by incorporating a text file to store the responses.

Run the following code on the board:

```
import random
import time

responses = ["yes","no","maybe"]
question = input("Ask me a question! > ")
time.sleep(2)
print(random.choice(responses))
```

Ask students to suggest some yes/no-type questions. After the third or fourth question, ask students how they think the game works. Draw out answers such as 'responses are randomly generated'. Explain to the students that the 8-ball is made up of 20 responses: ten positive, five negative and five neutral, e.g.:

Positive answers:
• It is certain • It is decidedly so
• Without a doubt • Yes
Negative answers:
• Don't count on it • My reply is no
• My sources say no
Neutral answers:
• Cannot predict now • Ask again later

Put the students into pairs (see Idea 1: Paired programming) and share the example solution. Challenge the students to code their own variation of the classic Magic 8-ball® game with all 20 responses.

Shakespearean insult generator

'Thou artless beef-witted barnacle!'

A great way to introduce lists and simple file-handling is for students to throw Shakespearean insults at one another!

Run this Python code on the board:

```
import random
column1=["artless", "bawdy", "beslubbering"]
column2=["base-court", "bat-fowling", "beef-witted"]
column3=["apple-john", "baggage", "barnacle"]
print("Thou " + random.choice(column1)
+ (" ") + random.choice(column2) + (" ") +
random.choice(column3))
```

Explain that the program works by selecting one word at random from each column (list) and combining them to make a random insult. You can find the full list at teachwithict.com/shakespearean-insult-generator. For example, if we were to take the first word from each of the three columns below, we would get 'Thou artless base-court apple-john'.

Column 1	Column 2	Column 3
artless	base-court	apple-john
bawdy	bat-fowling	baggage
beslubbering	beef-witted	barnacle

Have students start by creating a simple random name-selector:

```
import random
names = ["Bob", "Dave", "Stuart"]
print(random.choice(names))
```

Next, have students replace the last line with:

```
print("Minion" + " " + random.choice(names))
```

Finally, challenge students to create their own insult (or compliment) generator.

> **Teaching tip**
>
> You may wish to provide students with a template with the three lists already created. This will save the students from having to type all the words and reduce the chance of syntax errors. You can then ask the students to add a fourth list with alternative sentence starters, e.g. 'Thou', 'Thee', 'Ye Olde', etc.

IDEA 82

Chatting robot

'Can computers think?'

'Can computers think?' was a question posed by computer pioneer and artificial intelligence (AI) theorist Alan Turing. Turing proposed that, given time, a computer with sufficient computational power would acquire the abilities to rival human intelligence. A modern example of this is a chatbot (or chatting robot).

Teaching tip

Before attempting to program their own chatbot, share the sample code with the students and challenge them to 'break' or confuse the program and note down their findings.

Taking it further

Currently, every pause is exactly two seconds long, therefore making it obvious that the responses are from a computer and not a human. Challenge the students to add a random pause between each response.

Bonus idea ★

Have students create a list of responses from which the chatbot will pick at random.

Display the following thunk as the students enter the classroom: 'Can computers think?'. A thunk is a question with no right or wrong answer that literally stops you in your tracks and makes you think — for example, 'Does a hard disk weigh more when it's full?' or 'What colour would a zebra be if it lost all its stripes?' Direct students to the question on the board and allow them to digest and discuss this.

Run the following code on the board/screen (note: the following example is in Python but can easily be adapted for other programming languages):

```python
import time
name = input("Hello, what is your name? ")
time.sleep(2)
print("Hello " + name)
feeling = input("How are you today? ")
time.sleep(2)
if "good" in feeling.lower():
  print("I'm feeling good too!")
else:
  print("I'm sorry to hear that!")
```

Step through the code, explaining what each line is doing.

Put students into pairs (see Idea 1: Paired programming) and share the sample code from the board. Challenge the students to improve the sample program or create their own interpretation of the chatting robot (chatbot).

Just dance

'Sir, can we programme you to "floss"?'

Like a recipe or magic trick, dance is a great medium for introducing key programming concepts to children. Whether it's the latest 'Fortnite' dance or trending TikTok craze, dance can provide a great opportunity to contextualise learning!

Start by sharing with the class a simple dance routine in the form of an algorithm for them to act out. This could be a dance from popular culture or one that you have simply made up! For example:

```
Repeat 4 times
    Place hands on head
    Place hands on shoulders
    Place hands on knees
    Touch your toes
```

Next, open Scratch and select one of the sample dance sprites (D-Money Dance, Cassy Dance, Ten80 Dance, etc.). Demonstrate how to change a costume in Scratch (Looks → Switch costume to...) then share and run the following example code with students:

```
When ⚑ clicked
Repeat (10)
    Next costume
```

Ask the students what is wrong with the code. Draw out answers such as 'code is running too fast', etc. Add a one-second pause (Control → Wait 1 seconds) after 'Next costume' and run the code again. Explain that we need to add a pause to slow the code down.

Challenge the students to create a simple dance routine using any of the dance sprites in Scratch.

> **Bonus idea** ★
>
> Have students photograph each other performing different dance poses (preferably in front of a green or blue background) and upload their poses into Scratch.

Adventures in text

'You've reached a fork in the road! To the north there appears to be an ominous-looking cave. To the east you can see a creepy-looking forest.'

A great way to teach students how to use conditional (if/else/else if) statements and subroutines is to get them to write their own 80s-inspired 'text adventures'.

Teaching tip

Ask students to create a flowchart before coding their text adventure, so as to make the branching (decisions) a little easier to understand.

Run the following code on the board:

```
import time
required = ("\nPlease choose a, b, c etc.")

def start():
    print ("You've reached a fork in the road! "
    "To the north there is an ominous cave. "
    "To the east is a creepy-looking forest. "
    "Will you: ")
    time.sleep(1)
    print ("A. Take the north fork "
    "\nB. Take the east fork ")
    choice = input(">>> ")
    if choice.upper() == "A":
        cave()
    elif choice.upper() == "B":
        forest()
    else:
        print ("Please choose A or B!")
        start()

def cave():
    print ("\nAs you stand in front of the cave, "
    "a giant bear leaps out and strikes you "
    "down. GAME OVER!")
```

```
def forest():
    print ("\nAs you approach the forest, "
    "a giant snake appears from nowhere "
    "and bites you on the arm. GAME OVER!")

start()
```

Explain to the students how the code works, line by line.

Start by explaining that import time loads a built-in library in Python, which allows us to have natural pauses in the game and also allows us to add some suspense!

Explain that choice.upper() converts the player's answer to uppercase (a form of error-checking). Inform the students that by converting each of the player's answers to uppercase, we don't have to check for every possible variation of each response, e.g. 'A', 'a', 'B', 'b', etc.

Finally, highlight the importance of the def command. Explain that this is how we define a function in Python. Tell the students that they will be using functions to manage each of the different options/locations in their game.

Share the sample code (on page 102) with the students and challenge them to create their own text adventure. Time permitting, have students test out each other's adventure games.

Bonus idea ★

Have students modify their code in order to create a quiz.

Mad Libs®

'A great way to explore string manipulation in Python is to play a game of Mad Libs®!'

Mad Libs® is a phrasal template word game, usually played at parties, where one player prompts other players for a list of words to substitute blanks in a story before reading out the completed story aloud.

Taking it further

Challenge students to create a Mad Lib that contains two or more inputs. For example: 'I can't start my blank without my blank2!'

Start by running the following Python code on the board/screen:

```
phrase = "Rumble in the blank"
print(phrase)
noun = input("Enter a noun: ")
phrase = phrase.replace("blank", noun)
print(phrase)
```

Ask for volunteers to suggest words to replace the blank. If you wish, you could have the class vote on their favourite answer.

Inform students that a Mad Lib is a phrasal word game where players replace blanks in a phrase or story with a noun or place, etc. For example, the phrase 'Rumble in the blank' might end up as 'Rumble in the toilet'.

Explain to the students how the code works. In particular, explain that the line 'phrase = phrase.replace("blank", noun)' looks for the word 'blank' in the sentence and replaces it with the noun input by the player. Tell students that they will use the .replace() method to replace the blank(s) in their Mad Lib with the word(s) input by the user.

Bonus idea ★

Challenge students to create a list or file containing several phrases and modify their solution so that it picks a phrase from the file or list at random.

Challenge students to create their own Mad Libs® in Python. For example:

- 'It don't mean a thing if it ain't got that blank!'
- 'Rumble in the blank!'

Sorting Hat

'But I wanted to be in Slytherin!'

The Sorting Hat is an artefact used at Hogwarts in the *Harry Potter* books. The hat determines which of the four school houses (Gryffindor, Slytherin, Hufflepuff and Ravenclaw) each new student is assigned to. As well as introducing conditional (if/else) statements, the Sorting Hat is also great for exploring lists.

Start by running the following code on the board/screen:

```
import random
number = random.randint(1,4)
if number == 1:
  print("Gryffindor")
elif number == 2:
  print("Hufflepuff")
elif number == 3:
  print("Ravenclaw")
else:
  print("Slytherin")
```

Ask for some volunteers to come to the front of the class and sort them into their respective houses. Explain what each part of the program does and challenge the students to create their own Sorting Hat algorithm.

Once the students have finished coding their Sorting Hats, pose the question: 'What if we had more than four houses or we wanted to create a random name-selector with up to 30 names – what would be the problem with using an if/else/else if statement?' Draw out answers such as 'Easy to make mistakes' and 'Difficult to debug', etc. Share the following code and have students improve their solution:

```
import random
houses=["Slytherin", "Gryffindor",
  "Hufflepuff", "Ravenclaw"]
print(random.choice(houses))
```

Teaching tip

The example (left) is in Python but can easily be adapted for other programming languages.

Taking it further

Challenge students to create a random name-selector that will not select the same name more than once.

Turtle power (a lesson using PRIMM)

'A simple example that demonstrates the PRIMM approach.'

Using the turtle library in Python is a great way to help students to move from block-based languages such as Scratch to text-based languages like Python.

The following example uses the 'Turtle' library in Python but can be adapted for use with other applications such as Scratch, Logo, etc.

Predict
Share with students a working solution for creating a square using the Python turtle library. Challenge the students to draw (or act out) what they think the code will output.

Run
Run the code and compare the result with the students' predictions. Discuss with students their answers.

Investigate
Place the students into pairs and share with them the working solution. Task the students to comment or label the code to explain what each line is doing. Alternatively, ask students to explain a specific line of code.

Modify
Challenge the students to modify the code and investigate what happens. For example, the students could change the angle of turn, the distance the turtle travels or the number of times the code is repeated.

Make
Finally, challenge the students to use what they have learned to write a program to draw another regular polygon shape, such as an equilateral triangle, hexagon or octagon.

Bonus idea ★

Challenge the students to make their code more efficient by using loops (see Idea 3: Code golf).

Guess my number

'I'm thinking of a number...'

'Guess my number' is a great way to explore key programming concepts such as variables, data types and selection.

The computer will think of a random number between 1 and 20, and ask the player to guess it. The computer will inform the player whether each guess is too high or too low. The player wins if they can guess the number within six attempts.

Run the following code on the board/screen and ask for a volunteer to play the game:

```
import random
number = random.randint(1, 10)
name = input("What's your name? ")
number_of_guesses = 0
print(name + ", I'm thinking of a
number between 1 and 10")
while number_of_guesses < 5:
  guess = int(input("Guess? "))
  number_of_guesses += 1
  if guess < number:
    print("Too low")
  elif guess > number:
    print("Too high")
  else:
    break
if guess == number:
  print("You guessed right!")
else:
  print("Unlucky, the number was ")
  print(number)
```

Step through the code line by line, explaining how the program works, and challenge students to create their own 'guess my number' game.

> **Teaching tip**
>
> There is a lot going on for such a simple program. For that reason, it's recommended that you break up the program into small steps. I suggest starting with a fixed number before moving on to the random function.

Mind-reading algorithm

'Miss, can the computer really read my mind?'

This implementation of a simple 'mind-reading' trick is a great way to explore key programming concepts, as well as practising some string manipulation and basic mathematical operations.

Teaching tip

At the end of the activity, challenge students to create their own version of the game.

Taking it further

To make it look as if the computer is trying to read the player's mind, get students to add a random pause before revealing the answer:

```
import time
time.sleep(1)
```

Run the following code on the board and ask for a volunteer to play the game:

```
numberToAdd = 20
print("Think of a number between 1 and 20!")
input("Done? Press any key to continue.")
print("Double the number you're thinking of.")
input("Ready? Press any key to continue.")
print("Now, add " + str(numberToAdd))
input("Got it? Press any key to continue.")
print("Next, divide your answer by 2.")
input("Done? Press any key to continue.")
print("Now, take away the first number you "
"thought of.")
answer = numberToAdd / 2
print("Is your answer " + str(answer) + " ?")
```

Explain that the computer can't read people's minds but instead utilises a simple algorithm in which the answer will always be half the number you ask the player to add in step 3. Explain how the program works (line by line), paying particular attention to the str() function. Inform the students that because the variable 'numberToAdd' is an 'integer' (or number), before we can combine it with text, we must first convert it to a 'string'.

Inform students that there is a problem with this algorithm in that the answer will always be 10. Demonstrate how to use the random function to generate a random number:

```
import random
numberToAdd = random.randint(1,20)
```

Cat and mouse

'Engage your students with this fun introductory coding activity!'

For many young people, video games are an integral part of modern childhood, so it will not surprise you that having students create simple games with tools such as Scratch can be a great way to engage them with code!

Start by displaying the following code for a simple cat and mouse game on the screen/whiteboard. Ask the students to predict what will happen when the green flag is pressed:

when ⚐ clicked
forever
    point towards (mouse-pointer)
    move (5) steps

Put the students into pairs (see Idea 1: Paired programming) and challenge them to copy and tinker with the code. For example, the students could change the number of steps to see what effect it has on the game or change the sprite, etc.

Once the students are comfortable with how the code works, challenge them to add a conditional (IF) statement that displays a message when the cat sprite touches the cursor (catches the mouse).

Teaching tip

Encourage the students to talk their ideas through first before modifying their game. Provide them with individual whiteboards and pens if they want to write down their ideas.

Taking it further

Challenge students to improve their game further by adding extra features such as a countdown timer or scoring systems, or by adding obstacles (to create a maze game), etc.

Reaction timer

'Ready, steady, GO!'

This is a simple and fun activity to introduce the concept of variables.

Teaching tip

The example (right) is in Python but can easily be adapted for other programming languages.

Taking it further

Challenge the students to improve their game so that it runs the program more than once (loops) and keeps a record of the player's highest score.

Bonus idea ★

Have students add a conditional statement that ranks the player's speed – for example, if reaction time < 0.22 then print 'Greased lightning!' etc.

Start by running the following code on the board/screen:

```
import time, random
print("Ready...")
time.sleep(1)
print("Steady...")
time.sleep(2)
startTime = time.time()
input("GO!")
endTime = time.time()
reactionTime = endTime - startTime
print(reactionTime)
```

Step through the code, explaining what each line is doing, in particular lines 6, 8 and 9. Explain that these are called variables (a memory location used to store data) and that data held inside a variable can change or 'vary'.

Put students into pairs (see Idea 1: Paired programming) and have them replicate and run the code. Once the students have run the program a few times, ask them to place comments in the code explaining what each line is doing.

Next, instruct the students to replace line 5 'time.sleep(2)' with the following:

```
time.sleep(random.randint(2,5))
```

Ask the students to run the program again and explain what the new line of code is doing. Draw out answers such as 'adds a random pause between two and five seconds'.

Finally, have the students modify how the score is displayed, e.g.: print("Time: " + str(reactionTime) + " seconds").

Computing and STEAM

Part 10

Art attack

'Use art as a creative medium for exploring complex concepts in computing.'

As well as being fun and engaging, art can be a perfect medium for exploring complex concepts in computing.

Taking it further

Have students create a gallery of their masterpieces using PowerPoint or Sway, for example.

Pixel art

Binary representation of images
Have students create pixel art using binary, i.e. substitute white pixels with a 0 and black pixels with a 1. Students can add colour to their pixel art by creating 2-bit (four-colour) pixel art – for example, 00 = white, 01 = blue, 10 = yellow, 11 = black, etc. For extra stretch and challenge, have students share the binary representation of their image with a partner and challenge their partner to recreate the image (see Idea 64).

Minecraft
Minecraft (Raspberry Pi Edition) and Minecraft: Education Edition now allow you to place blocks using code. Have students create pixel art in Minecraft using Python, JavaScript or Microsoft MakeCode.

Turtle graphics

Have students create turtle art using the Turtle library in Python or Scratch or dedicated turtle drawing app. Alternatively, you could adapt an existing programmable robot (for example, adding a pen or paintbrush) and program it to draw on a large piece of paper (see Idea 87).

Paint bot

Don't mind getting a little messy? Some programmable robots, such as Sphero, are waterproof, while others have dedicated brush/pen attachments. Have students create modern-day masterpieces using water-based paints and a very large canvas.

Lights, camera, action

'Sir, this is literally the coolest thing ever!'

You may have seen examples of slow shutter speed photography (when a camera's shutter is open for longer to allow in more light) such as 'light painting' or 'motion blur'. Thankfully, you don't need an expensive camera to create your own slow shutter speed artwork.

What you will need

- a camera (or phone/tablet) that allows you to adjust the shutter speed
- a programmable device that emits colour, e.g. Sphero
- a dark room.

How it works

- Have students program their robot to create a simple pattern, such as their first initial or a regular polygon.
- Turn off the camera's flash.
- Adjust the ISO (this defines how sensitive the sensor is to light). Set this to the lowest setting possible (usually between 50 and 100). If you have this too high, you run the risk of overexposing/having too much light and ending up with a bright white image.
- Set the camera's shutter speed to the longest setting (anything between 10 and 30 seconds). Needless to say, the longer the exposure you choose, the more time the sensor is exposed to light and the longer the light trail will be.
- Lower the lights.
- Take the photo.

When creating slow shutter speed artwork, it is highly recommended that you use a tripod. If using a mobile device, use a stand or tripod mount that is compatible with your device.

Making music

'Having students create music with code is just one creative approach to engaging them with computer science!'

Music is the perfect medium for introducing key programming concepts such as sequence, iteration and subroutines, but where do you start and how do you combine the two mediums without it being just a tenuous link?

Taking it further

Put students into pairs (see Idea 1: Paired programming) and ask them to transpose sheet music for popular songs, such as Frère Jacques or Baby Shark, using code.

Method 1: Sonic Pi

Sonic Pi (sonic-pi.net) is an open-source program, based on the Ruby programming language, that lets you compose and perform music with code.

What makes Sonic Pi so appealing is that the syntax is very forgiving; this makes it an ideal first text-based language, especially for those wishing to move from blocks to text.

As well as introducing children to key concepts such as algorithm design, variables, iteration, etc., Sonic Pi also introduces children to concepts such as multi-threading (playing sequences simultaneously), randomisation, parameters and live coding.

Method 2: Musical algorithms

By taking advantage of the sound blocks in Scratch, children can create their own musical compositions. To play a note in Scratch, we use the following command:

Play note 60 for 0.5 seconds

In this case, 60 is the note (Middle C) and 0.5 is the duration.

Students can take things further by playing multiple scripts at the same time, for example, to create chords, or by attaching scripts to different sprites to create virtual instruments.

Method 3: Physical computing

Sound is created by vibrations in air. The number of vibrations per second is called the frequency, and frequency is measured in Hertz (Hz). A musical note is essentially an audio signal at a specific frequency – for example, C4 (Middle C) is equivalent to 256.87 Hz. If you know the frequency of the notes you want to play, you can start to compose a melody.

When attaching a speaker or buzzer to a physical computing device such as Arduino, Micro:bit or Raspberry Pi, for example, it is possible to simulate musical notes by specifying the frequency of the attached buzzer. Trying to remember each frequency can be a challenge but this can easily be remedied by creating variables to store the frequency of each note. It is also possible to use lists (arrays) to store each sequence of notes. For this reason, I find that music is great for exploring the purpose of variables and lists. Note: Some programming environments, such as MicroPython (see example below), conveniently map each of the notes for us. Example:

```
tune = ["c4:4", "d4:4", "e4:4", "c4:4", "c4:4",
    "d4:4", "e4:4", "c4:4", "e4:4", "f4:4", "g4:8",
    "e4:4", "f4:4", "g4:8"]
```

In this case, C = note, 4 = octave and :4 = duration (beat or ticks).

Using notes rather than frequencies provides a layer of abstraction that makes it easier for children to identify sounds that can be used to make music. Lists provide a way to group together the sounds to create a sequence in order to produce a melody.

Bonus idea ★

Have students code a piece of music to accompany an animation or video.

IDEA 95

Coding probability

'I thought this was meant to be a computing lesson, not a maths lesson!'

Computer science and mathematics are closely linked; in fact, early computer science was strongly influenced by the work of mathematicians such as Alan Turing, John von Neumann and Rózsa Péter. So it's not surprising that computer science offers numerous cross-curricular opportunities for exploring mathematics.

Taking it further

Challenge the students to create a dice simulator and work out the relative frequency of the dice landing on a six.

Remind students that 'probability' is the measure of how likely it is that something will happen, and that the chance of an event happening can be described in words – for example, 'certain', 'likely' or 'impossible'. Inform the students that probability is often represented as a fraction – for example, the probability of getting 'tails' when you flip a coin is a one in two chance, or ½. Explain that probability can also be shown as a decimal or percentage – for example, a probability of ½ can also be shown as 0.5 or 50 per cent.

Share the following example code for a simple 'coin flip' game (note: the following example is in Python but can easily be adapted for other programming languages such as Scratch or JavaScript):

```
import random
coin = random.randrange(2)
if coin == 0:
    print("Heads")
else:
    print("Tails")
```

Challenge the students to run the code ten times, each time keeping a tally of how many times the coin lands on 'heads' or 'tails'.

116

Inform the students that the theoretical probability of getting a 'heads' when flipping a coin is ½; however, if a coin was actually flipped several times, you may get more heads than tails. Explain that 'relative frequency' (or experimental probability) is calculated by dividing the number of times an event occurs by the total number of trials in an experiment, and that relative frequency is used when probability is being estimated using the outcomes of an experiment or trial. Ask the students to calculate the relative frequency for their coin flip test.

Tell the students that in order to improve the accuracy of the results, we would need to run the experiment several times. Explain that this is one of the advantages of using a computer simulation!

Share the following example code:

```
import random
heads = 0
for x in range(0, 100):
  coin = random.randrange(2)
  if coin == 0:
    print("Heads")
    heads +=1
  else:
    print("Tails")
print("Number of heads: ")
print(heads)
```

Have the students replicate the code and modify it so that it calculates and displays the relative frequency of the coin landing on 'heads'.

Possible solution:

```
probability = (heads / 100)
print("Probability of heads = " + str(probability))
```

Bonus idea ★

Have the students display their answer as a percentage by multiplying it by 100.

Physical computing

'Context is key when teaching computing, so make sure that what you teach is relatable to your students!'

Many concepts in computing can be very abstract, which presents a huge challenge for learners who are new to the subject. Physical computing connects these concepts to something concrete, which can both engage learners and provide a 'real-world' context for why they are learning to code.

Teaching tip

I suggest starting to explore physical computing as part of a club or enrichment activity. This way you can find out what works and what doesn't, discover what engages your students and test out your ideas before adapting them for the classroom.

Physical computing, put simply, is the interaction between physical 'real-world' objects and the 'virtual' computer environment. Physical computing interactions are all around us in our everyday lives, from smart homes and smartphones to assembly lines and driverless vehicles. Behind each of these applications are algorithms and programs that govern their behaviour.

In the classroom, physical computing can manifest itself as something as simple as turning on an LED or powering up a motor to something a little more challenging, such as building a wearable computer.

Similar to robotics, learners can immediately see the result of their code and more easily identify when their code is not working.

Turtle snowflakes

'Let it go!'

Have students channel their inner 'Elsa' by creating snowflakes in Python.

Start by running the following code to draw a parallelogram on the board/screen:

```
import turtle
elsa = turtle.Turtle()
for i in range(2):
    elsa.forward(100)
    elsa.right(60)
    elsa.forward(100)
    elsa.right(120)
```

Teaching tip

To work out the final angle, use the formula: 360 / number of iterations, e.g. if the number of iterations is 4 'for i in range(4)', then 360 / 4 = 90 degrees, so the last instruction would be 'elsa.right(90)'.

Challenge the students to predict what shape the code will draw. Run the program and compare the result with the students' predictions.

Inform the students that we can put loops inside other loops and share the following example:

```
import turtle
elsa = turtle.Turtle()
for i in range(4):
  for j in range(2):
    elsa.forward(100)
    elsa.right(60)
    elsa.forward(100)
    elsa.right(120)
    elsa.right(90)
```

Put the students into pairs (see Idea 1: Paired programming) and instruct them to copy the code. Challenge the students to tinker with the code, changing the number of iterations 'for i in range(4)' and final angle 'elsa.right(90)', to see who can create the 'coolest' snowflake!

Coding the weather

'Cloudy with a chance of 1s and 0s.'

Computer science is everywhere, but it's not always obvious where it's being applied. By giving students access to 'real' data, such as weather data, they will be able to see connections between computer science and other disciplines, such as — in this scenario — meteorology and weather forecasting.

Taking it further

Challenge the students to convert the temperature from Kelvin to degrees Celsius using the formula below:
Celsius = Kelvin - 273.15

We can access live weather data for over 200,000 cities worldwide using OpenWeatherMap API. To use OpenWeatherMap API, you will first need to create a free account.

Step 1
- Go to openweathermap.org and sign up.
- Sign in and click on 'API Keys'.

Step 2
Visit repl.it (https://repl.it/languages/python3). repl.it is a free (no sign-up), collaborative, in-browser IDE supporting more than 50 languages, including Python.

Step 3
Run the following code on the board/screen. Note: Ensure that you copy and paste the API key, from the previous step, before running the code.

```
import requests

API_key = "Insert the API Key inside these quotes"

base_url = "http://api.openweathermap.org/data/2.5/weather?"

city_name = input("Enter city name : ")

# full url = base url + app key + city name.
```

```
full_url = base_url + "appid=" + API_key +
"&q=" + city_name

weather_data = requests.get(full_url).json()

# JSON data works similarly to a Python
# dictionary and can be accessed using
# square brackets [].

# Temperature is located in ["main"] in the
# key ["temp"]
temp = weather_data["main"]["temp"]

wind_speed = weather_data["wind"]["speed"]

description = weather_data["weather"][0]
["description"]

print("\nTemperature : ",temp)
print("\nWind Speed : ",wind_speed)
print("\nDescription : ",description)
```

Step through the code line by line, explaining what each line is doing. Put the students into pairs (see Idea 1: Paired programming) and have them replicate and run the code before modifying their program to include more weather data (see below).

```
Location = weather_data["name"]
MaxTemp = weather_data["main"]["temp_max"]
MinTemp = weather_data["main"]["temp_min"]
Humidity = weather_data["main"]["humidity"]
Pressure = weather_data["main"]["pressure"]
```

Bonus idea ★

Have the students record a weather report (with a green screen) using the data from OpenWeatherMap.

IDEA 99

Rubbish robots

'If *Blue Peter* ever did *Robot Wars*!'

One of my favourite physical computing projects is called 'junk modelling'. As the name suggests, in junk modelling, students are challenged to build and code a robot, vehicle or contraption (think *Wallace and Gromit* or Heath Robinson) using a combination of regular household objects (milk cartons, plastic straws, cardboard tubes, etc.) and electronic components (LEDs, motors, servos and buzzers). A popular variation of the junk modelling approach is 'Rubbish robots'.

Teaching tip

I find that having a narrative (or back story) helps to provide a context for the learning activity and provides a focus for when the students are designing their robots.

Bonus idea ★

Have students design and build an add-on for an existing robot (Sphero, Dash, etc.), such as a robotic arm or pen-holder, out of regular household objects.

How it works

Start by setting the scene. For example: A truck carrying hazardous material has overturned, spilling all of its contents over a busy highway.

Provide students with a selection of everyday household items (washing-up liquid bottles, cartons, cardboard boxes, etc.), as well as some adhesive tape, scissors, glue, etc. to help the students assemble their robots. Also provide a selection of components, such as LEDs, motors, servos and buzzers for the students to use in their build.

Inform the students that they have been challenged to create a robot, using the materials provided, to move (push, pull, scoop, etc.) the hazardous material to a safe location.

Students can use whatever device they have available to control their 'Rubbish robot' (Arduino, Micro:bit, CodeBug, Raspberry Pi, etc.) and are allowed to use either a blocks-based or text-based programming language.

Colour splash

'Make your images stand out by adding a splash of colour!'

Colour splash is a technique in which a 'splash of colour' is added to a black and white photo to create a dramatic contrasting effect that draws the audience's attention to the subject/area that you want to emphasise. The effect is synonymous with festive cards (robin or red letterbox surrounded by snow), as the splash of red colour creates a striking contrast with the white background.

Start by asking students what they think of when they hear the word 'filter'. Draw out answers such as Snapchat, Instagram, etc. Share some examples of 'colour splash' images sourced from the internet – for example, London bus, New York taxi, child with balloons, etc. Inform students that the two most commonly used filters are 'contrast' and 'brightness'. Explain that by changing the contrast, the image will appear duller or more vibrant and that by changing the brightness, the image will appear lighter or darker.

Using your chosen image-editing software (Photoshop, GIMP, pixlr.com, etc.), demonstrate how to create a colour splash image.

Instructions

1 Find a suitable image (see examples in the description above).
2 Add the selected image as a new layer in your chosen software.
3 Create a new layer containing a duplicate of the selected image.
4 Add a black and white filter to the original (background) layer.
5 Remove the background from the top layer using either the eraser or the selection tool (slowly revealing the black and white background layer).

> **Teaching tip**
>
> As well as Introducing filters and layers, this activity is perfect for exploring Creative Commons. Have the students source Creative Commons images for their 'colour splash' creations and attribute the images appropriately.

> **Taking it further**
>
> Place students into pairs and challenge them to create their own colour splash images using images sourced from the internet.